THOUSAND TIMES BROKEN

THOUSAND TIMES BROKEN

Three Books

~

Henri Michaux

Translated from the French
by Gillian Conoley

City Lights Books | San Francisco

Copyright © 2001 Editions Gallimard
English language translation © 2014 Gillian Conoley

First published as *Quarte cents hommes en croix* by Pierre Bettencourt in 1956, *Paix dans les brisements* by Éditions Flinker in 1959, and *Vigies sur cibles* by Éditions du Dragon in 1959.

First City Lights Books edition, 2014

Cover art: Henri Michaux

Gratitude and thanks to magazines and editors who published excerpts of these translations: David Bonanno, Stephen Berg, and Elizabeth Scanlon, *American Poetry Review*; Bradford Morrow, *Conjunctions*; Maxine Chernoff and Paul Hoover, *New American Writing*; Claudia Keelan, *Interim*; Mitch Taylor, *The Ancients*; and Joshua Marie Wilkinson, *The Volta*.

Library of Congress Cataloging-in-Publication Data
Michaux, Henri, 1899-1984.
 [Works. Selections. English]
 Thousand times broken : three books / Henri Michaux ; translated from the French by Gillian Conoley.
    pages cm
 ISBN 978-0-87286-648-5 (paperback)
 1. Experimental fiction, French. I. Conoley, Gillian, 1955- translator. II. Title.
 PQ2625.I2A2 2014
 841'.912—dc23
                                2014023851

City Lights Books are published at the City Lights Bookstore, 261 Columbus Avenue, San Francisco, CA 94133
www.citylights.com

CONTENTS

INTRODUCTION

These three titles were all written between 1956 and 1959, during Henri Michaux's 11-year, on-again, off-again experiment with mescaline. Each is at once a departure from and a continuation of the Michaux we know, if one can say one can "know" Michaux—a writer and visual artist who marked little difference between the machinations of our internal and external worlds, and who viewed both as forces we should somehow throw off, exorcise, excise. The self? An impediment. World? Apparition. Language, marks, drawings, paintings? Failures, and with agendas of their own. Only the unknown, and within the unknown, only the uncontrollable, might be trusted.

Both Michaux's writing and visual art are marked by two obsessions: to delve into the darker, shadowy realms of human consciousness, and to record what he saw in the most scrupulous, exacting fashion he could muster, whether it be through language or drawing, with India ink (his most preferred medium), watercolor, or paint. Throughout, one can trace the struggle for, and his disappointment in not finding, a medium up to the task, or a universal language through gesture, mark, sign, and the word.

Never wavering from continual journeys into perception and consciousness throughout the almost 60 years of his creative life, Belgian-born Henri Michaux (1899-1984) was one of the most influential French writers and visual artists of the twentieth century. Difficult to classify, he was often linked to the surrealists, an identification he eschewed. Michaux published over thirty books of poems, narratives, essays, travelogues, journals, and drawings. His visual work—almost eclipsing his reputation as a writer—was shown in major museums of Europe and the United States, including the Guggenheim in New York, and the Musée d'Art Moderne in Paris.

In each of these three books, correspondences between the verbal and the pictorial become more pronounced, more urgent and dramatic than anywhere else within Michaux's entire oeuvre. We see the crucifix as icon appear as a broken mark or alphabetic letter. The human eye sprouts a watchtower whose "target" is either object or subject or some netherworld in between. A fluid, torrential "vibratile carpet" appears like an unending page on which word and image fly.

MYSTICISM AND MESCALINE

As a young man, Michaux immersed himself in mystical literature (Ruysbroeck, Pascal, Ernest Hello, Lao-Tse) to find "the same fugitive and contourless universe" of his experience. Michaux's shifts between external and internal stimuli can often be dizzying. Many have commented on the somatic, bodily experience the writing of Michaux can induce. One of his earliest translators, Richard Ellman, explained, "Reading Michaux makes one uncomfortable . . . if we try to reassure ourselves by calling it fantasy, we have to ignore the scalpel which is playing about our insides" (Ellman 14).

As in all his work, in these three books we find Michaux seeking to wrestle himself from the familiarity of his own consciousness through an adopted or induced experience: travel, mescaline, journeys into imagined worlds of creatures or beasts, Western or Eastern spirituality. These ventures into consciousness are relentlessly explored from his first book to his last, including the early *My Properties* (1929), the half-imaginary travel journals of *A Barbarian in Asia* (1933), the invented lands and mythical animals of *Elsewhere* (1948), the mescaline-induced textual columns and frenetic drawings of *Misérable miracle* (1956), and the mystical expeditions into Buddhism, Hinduism, and tantric art in *The Exalted Garden* (1984).

Throughout each exploration, one becomes aware of a split in consciousness. While there is a mind at play, courting chaos, there is also a mind acutely observant and vigilant, taking note of every synapse, each glimmer of the unknown. As much as Michaux is desirous of vision, he is desirous to chart the course. While the work is strange, dark, and fantastic, his stance is often scientific, rational, that of one who is taking account, detached. Thus, Michaux, who once attended medical school, is both "poetic" and "scientific" at the same time, taking Rimbaud's statement: "contemporary poetry can no longer content itself with vague lyricism, but only with total self-knowledge," quite seriously.

Michaux's goal, however—like Rimbaud's—was not to arrive at a more extensive personal self-knowledge, but to prove a more intimate contact with human consciousness available to those who brave it. "Communicate?" Michaux would ask in the aphoristic book *Tent Poles*, where the pronoun referent is left ambiguously open—either Michaux himself, the reader, or yet another—"You too would like to communicate? Communicate what?. . .You're not intimate enough with you, poor fool, to have something to communicate" (Michaux, *Tent Poles* 97). And similarly, he would ask, "However weighed down, washed-up, bullied you may be, ask yourself regularly—and irregularly—'What can I risk again today?'" (*Tent Poles* 85).

It should be made clear that Michaux was far from an addict, and only took mescaline a handful of times over the course of the 11-year experiment. A teetotaler most of his life, Michaux began experimenting with mescaline sometime around 1954-55, when a neurologist friend encouraged him to try the drug. Michaux, apparently reluctant at first, was drawn to mescaline for its capacity to enhance a more precise division in consciousness he was already experiencing in his art, a state in which one part of the brain remains unillusioned and lucid during vision, fantasy, or hallucination.

Michaux himself has often been referred to as a substance. John Ashbery, in a preface to a 1961 interview he conducted with Michaux in Paris, described him as "hardly a painter, hardly even a writer, but a conscience—the most sensitive substance yet discovered for registering the fluctuating anguish of day-to-day, minute-to-minute living" (Ashbery 396). Octavio Paz, in an introduction to *Misérable miracle*, wrote, "When I had read the last page, I asked myself whether the result of the experiment had not been precisely the opposite: the poet Michaux explored by mescaline" (Michaux, *Misérable miracle* ix).

Quitting entirely at age 67, Michaux reportedly did not "like" the drug: "Should one speak of pleasure? It was unpleasant." By 1961, Michaux writes: "Drugs bore us with their paradises. Let them give us a little knowledge instead. This is not a century for paradise." Writing to his friend Octavio Paz, Michaux explains: "Devotees of the simple perspective may be tempted to judge all my writings as those of a drug addict. I regret to say that I am more the water-drinking type."

EARLIER VISUAL/VERBAL EXPERIMENTS

Questions of perception and representation—the blur between the visual and the verbal—have early roots in Michaux, with the publication of *Entre centre et absence* (1936) and the later *Peintures* (1939), *Labyrinthes* (1944), *Peintures et dessins* (1946), *Apparitions* (1946), *Meidosems* (1948), and *Mouvements* (1951). In the first editions of each of these books, Michaux placed his original artwork next to his writing. On each title page, the visual works were described as being "illustrations of the author," which resulted in these texts falling into the category of "illustrated books," though Michaux never had the intention that the poems act as texts for the visual, nor that the visual stand as illustration for the texts. Instead, these books lay

the early groundwork for a dialog between the visual and the verbal in which Michaux sought to create a dynamic, rather than subordinate, interaction.

Michaux's earliest visual works (made around the same time as his first serious literary work) were ink drawings titled "Narration" and "Alphabet." Art critic and poet Barry Schwabsky, writing in *Artforum*, describes the work as suggestive of texts "handwritten in characters that only appear once, if such a thing were possible." From the outset of his creative life, we see Michaux trying to "draw" a new language. Schwabsky explains, "Michaux's draftsmanship was born out of an urge to depict the strangeness of writing—to produce something even more opaque than the invented words in his poems of the period, just as those words amplify the vivifying effect he had found as a child of isolated words in the dictionary, where 'words . . . do not yet belong to phrases, to phrasemakers'" (*Artforum* 42).

In 1956, Michaux would write one of the earliest of what would become six mescaline texts: the multi-columned *Misérable miracle,* accompanied by the discordant drawings and illegible, gestural handwriting produced under the drug's influence. Later in his life, in the 1960s-1970s, he would move restlessly between line, color and rhythm in both his poetic and visual art, and begin to work from the model of the Chinese ideogram, ultimately transmuting it into a new language of pure lines. In these pen and ink drawings, the human figure takes on the gestural aspect of the handwritten letter, and simultaneously seems to be running toward the next, in horizontal lines running left to right, as in an alphabetical text. Increasingly, letter, sign, and mark appear as human figure.

FOUR HUNDRED MEN ON THE CROSS

Four Hundred Men on the Cross is perhaps Henri Michaux's most haunting and enigmatic text, one in which we see

Michaux's life-long quest to fuse the visual and the verbal taking on a new trajectory. Appearing in 1956, between publication of the first two books written during the mescaline experiments—*Misérable miracle* (1956) and *L'Infini turbulent* (1957)—*Four Hundred Men on the Cross* is the only book in which we see Michaux shaping poems into object-like figures, creating a simultaneous, rather than complementary, visual and verbal experience.

Four Hundred Men on the Cross is a series of quick, fleeting portraits of the crucifixion, wherein Michaux presents the human body as an image that can no longer find corollary with myth and metamorphosis. Again and again, Michaux tries to render Christ on the cross, but cannot seem to get him to stay put, either through language or drawing.

Noting that the exact date of composition of *Four Hundred Men on the Cross* remains a mystery (whether Michaux wrote the book just before or just after he first took mescaline is unknown), Bellour suggests that in this writing Michaux is preparing the human body for further experiment in the mescaline texts. Bellour calls "this enigmatic book a perfect transition to the books about drugs" and contends that in this text, Michaux leaves behind the invented suffering body of his earlier work, and replaces it with "a body that has become experimental, biological and physical, offering itself to question thought, with no further detours" (Michaux *Œuvres complètes* 1326).

In his depictions of the human body on the cross, Michaux begins to meld the two worlds of the pictorial and the poetic, tracing a shifting universe of verbal and visual signification found within and between the graphic images of his printed texts and the gestural expressivity of his drawings. In the opening pages, the shifting font sizes and shaping of fragments give the poems a sense of objecthood or sign, which Michaux then takes a step further, as the poems themselves become the cross, or a text hiding the infant Christ, or a Christ figure floating in air.

Three pen and ink drawings of the crucifixion also appear in the book; the other drawings, to which the writing ostensibly refers, Michaux leaves absent. In *Four Hundred Men on the Cross*, the reader/viewer must continually shift foci between reading and seeing. While seeking to regain his lost faith, Michaux is also asking, "What is reading? What is seeing?"

Margaret Rigaud-Drayton, writing in her groundbreaking *Henri Michaux: Poetry, Painting and the Universal Sign*, explains, "It is in the experimental *Quatre cents hommes en croix* that Michaux goes the furthest in graphic writing . . . its typographically unconventional fragments take on the function of visual signs, even as they remain discursively legible texts . . . they transcend the opposition between 'to show and name; to appear and say; to reproduce and articulate; to imitate and mean; to look at and read' somewhat as calligrams do according to Foucault" (Rigaud-Drayton 148).

In *Four Hundred Men on the Cross*, Michaux grapples with his lost faith by trying to write and draw the crucified Christ, the model through which the self can only try to conform, bound to failure. Writing and drawing become a substitute for belief. The "draftsman" in the text eventually multiplies into many draftsmen, mirroring the multiple crucified beings represented both visually and verbally—creating a sort of pictorial/poetic house of mirrors in which Christ refuses to appear or remain.

With this book, Michaux aligns himself within the long and continuing tradition of the malleable form of the auto portrait through Christ, joining Saint Augustine, Montaigne, Dante, Rousseau, Nietzsche (and closer to us, Roland Barthes, and among filmmakers, Federico Fellini, Carl Theodor Dreyer, Martin Scorsese, and Jean-Luc Goddard), each of whom—in various ways—depicted the passion of the self transmuted through the crucified Christ.

Shifting in typography between different fonts and

font sizes and the direction of its print, *Four Hundred Men on the Cross* contains discontinuously numbered poems and fragments which nevertheless move forward much in the same way a person of Catholic faith walks through the stations of the cross toward resurrection. In both drawing and writing Christ on the cross—the crucifixion itself a sign—Michaux seeks to somehow reunite himself with an earlier, profound faith experienced in adolescence and early adulthood.

As a young man Michaux wanted to join the priesthood, but was dissuaded by his father, a Catholic lawyer, who preferred he become a doctor. Born in Namur, educated at Putte-Grasheide and a Jesuit school in Brussels, Michaux began medical studies at Brussels University, but eventually rebelled against his parents' wishes, dropped out, and traveled North and South America as a ship's stoker in the French Merchant Marines. In 1923 he moved to Paris, supported himself by working as a teacher and secretary, and began to paint and write. In 1925, Michaux wrote, "I love without restriction nor explanation: Lautréamont and Ernest Hello. In all honesty, Christ as well" (Michaux *Œuvres complètes* 1319).

Thirty years later, we find Michaux, now accomplished as both a writer and an artist, working the tools of both mediums in an effort to return to his earlier experiences with Christ. We also find Michaux, in reference to his lost faith, being uncharacteristically eloquent: "United with Him, surrounded by images of Him on the cross, finding all meaningful life in Him, through Him, with Him, in preference to all other beings on earth, but that was long ago, that was in the serious years of my life, in my adolescence. . . ." (Michaux *Œuvres complètes* 802).

Upon completion of *Four Hundred Men on the Cross,* Michaux wrote to his friend, the French writer, critic and publisher Jean Paulhan. In this note, Michaux explains that the two blank pages he inserts toward the end of the

text are there to indicate the 30-year time lapse between Michaux's faith and this writing. The note also refers to the importance of Christ to Michaux:

> As for the man on the cross, he's completely stopped being interesting to me since the last drawings. After I described these last ones, it seemed to me that if I didn't add how important He was to me, I wouldn't be able to make people understand anything about me. So the extra pages were strictly for other people; restoring me to the state I was in thirty years before, for them. Restoring me too much. I never knew how to compose! But there was no morning after. Everything was truly in the grave.
>
> (Michaux *Œuvres complètes* 1321).

While English language critics and translators often mention Michaux's interest in and use of Eastern spirituality, especially as found in *The Exalted Garden*, one of the last works Michaux published before his death in 1984, scant mention is made of Michaux's conflicted relationship with Christianity, and in particular, the Christ figure. For this, I would direct the reader to Bellour's extensive commentary in the Gallimard edition of Michaux's *Œuvres complètes*. In *Four Hundred Men on the Cross*, on the title page, Henri Michaux literally nails his name to the cross, and begins another journey to the infinite.

WATCHTOWERS ON TARGETS

Watchtowers on Targets, published in 1959, two years after *L'Infini turbulent,* and three years after *Misérable miracle,* is a collaboration with Chilean abstract surrealist Roberto Matta, the painter with whom Michaux felt the closest affinity. Matta and Michaux set up the following rules for

their project: for the first two sections, Michaux would respond to Matta's etchings, and for the third, Matta would work from Michaux's writing. With its quick starts and abrupt stops in narrative, and without the overall narrative arc—however tentative—one usually sees in Michaux, the book is unusual within Michaux's oeuvre. Early on, a crime is committed, but this storyline vanishes, only to be replaced by characters, beasts, and insects who appear unannounced, often disappearing as quickly as they appear. What remains central throughout the book is the activity of the eye in the flux of perception, in the rapid-fire correspondence between the visual and the verbal as supplied by Matta and Michaux.

Watchtower on Targets' title enacts the ever shifting, tilted perspective of the book: a watchman, who, from his observation post, also becomes the target of observation, so that the very activity of "watching" turns back upon itself. The book is unedited and unrevised, most likely to keep the quick pace of response between Michaux and Matta intact. As though in continual correspondence, the whirlwind qualities of Matta's etchings and Michaux's quickly shifting verbal tableaus create a sense of upended spinning and multiplying that only ceases with the book's last line, "*Sun that is able to reunite.*" This final line, which declares a re-stitching, or coming back together of the sun, Michaux takes care to italicize, to indicate a repair of, or response to, "sun's slit throat," the infamous last line in Apollinaire's great poem "Zone."

The middle section, "Correspondence," is the only epistolary writing Michaux was to create. Playing with both the visual and verbal qualities of a postcard—and with its qualities of being "sent" and "received" within a correspondence—Michaux uses the word "card" in naming each of the six sections he also numbers in sequence. This distinct, separate quality of each "card" draws attention to the individual world Michaux builds within each correspondence.

In response, Matta presents each of Michaux's "four observers" folded over the image of a playing card. The four observers, seated at a card table, are as intent upon the card as object as they are upon the spinning world of their own individual psyches, all while simultaneously concentrating on the activity of exchange in a game of cards.

In his notes on *Watchtowers on Targets* in *Œuvres complètes*, Raymond Bellour writes: "Actions and accidents, codes and phenomena crop up, making themselves known and disappearing just like dead stars . . ."

It remains unknown whether it was Michaux or Matta who created the title, but Matta, who died in 2002, 18 years after Michaux, often spoke of how, years after their collaboration, he experienced Michaux's writing still "playing around in his head." Matta explained, "Death interrupted me, I was counting so much on his presence, on the watchman. He was vigilant against my enthusiasm that could be a little too spontaneous at times, he restrained me and that was friendship. Now I am an orphan of this vigilance and I am becoming a target exposed to everything."

PEACE IN THE BREAKING

Peace in the Breaking, the fourth of Michaux's mescaline texts, appeared in 1959. In this book, Michaux continues to explore both the furrow shape from *Misérable miracle* (1956) and the practice of the "endless poem" in *L'Infini turbulent* (1957). The text begins with spine-like, seismographic drawings that grow bigger and wider until they no longer form anything but a dust of signs, with the last page containing only the small beats of wings without birds. The poem, also shaped into a furrow-like spine, traces the shocks and sensation of being, the blockages and accelerations of rhythms and senses. Noting the rapid occasional rises that run through many of Michaux's poems, ascensions that appear then quickly dissipate, critic Reinhard

Kuhn writes that in *Peace in the Breaking*, a peak or point of rupture, "an upward slope" or "simple unstoppable ascent" is sustained for the first time, a gesture "that modifies not only the direction but the substance itself of Michaux's poetic enterprise" (Kuhn 190).

In *Peace in the Breaking*, not only do the title poem and drawings find formal corollary, but also the constraint of book as object begins to break down. The book is composed of four parts: drawings, two essay-like prose pieces, and poetry, all unrolling in a vertical, kakemono-like shape similar to the Chinese or Japanese scroll—and imitating, in its descending/ascending form, the drug experience from which the book was born.

As Raymond Bellour explains in Michaux's *Œuvres complètes*, the visual format of the original book appeared "*a l' italienne*, (on the smallest side of the rectangle) . . . so that the book is read vertically, as a notepad, with the binding on top and not on the left." The effect was one of a continual stream. Bellour continues: "So much so that one hesitates to talk about six or twelve mescaline drawings to evoke the twelve pages they cover. These drawings, in fact, are read or are seen two at a time, each time according to the continuity of the two pages opened together. . . One tends to forget the gaps in the motif in order to feel the dominant effect: a single drawing that unfolds as though it were endless until its final disappearance or evanescence, an immense dorsal spine, a central furrow around which words gather."

Desiring a "volume with a single page infinitely refolded," Michaux called both the drawings and the poem "leashes of reflections" (a term which, as Bellour points out, brings up notions of anchorage at sea, or links or furrows in the space defined by the oscillation of tides, or a wave's "breaking"). Throughout what Michaux called "the involuntary evocations" of either drawing or poetry, he invites the reader to enter his vision of "a nervous projection

screen," or "vibratile carpet," over which images or visualized words pass.

If we view *Four Hundred Men on the Cross* as a preparation of the body for the mescaline experiments, then in *Peace in the Breaking* we see Michaux, with the assistance of mescaline, freeing himself of the unwieldy body. Michaux once said, "I wish I could paint man when out of himself, paint his space." One also thinks of Michaux's statement: "True poetry will always belong to those who were looking for something beyond the human, who strove to dominate and overtake it . . . it will belong to the great scientists, the mystics . . ." (*Œuvre complètes* 1368). Present throughout *Peace in the Breaking* is what Maurice Blanchot called "the pure vibrating emanation of presence." Most significantly, in the title poem "Peace in the Breaking," the rational and the irrational mind unite, the only time this occurs in Michaux's oeuvre, through pure ascension.

Alain Jouffroy once asked Michaux about the compositional process of *Peace in the Breaking* with the double question: "how are images that later form your drawings born within you" and "how was the poem that your internal vision suggested to you born afterwards?" Michaux responds:

> The rolling, effervescent passage, the same passage of being itself, in its incessantly colliding continuation, there is what is drawn then within an abrupt silence, and, some time later, either well or badly, from a memory still freshly etched.
>
> In the storm without water, sometimes in an immense, settled, undulating cloth, the words appear, stammering visionary rags of a lost knowledge, all new, which the accident renders blindly clear.
>
> Words and drawings both come out of the capsizing. But of an inapparent and profound

capsizing they will come out insolently, days and weeks later, word-buoys of strange, unequal return. But more pushed, more "returning."

Michaux also called "Peace in the Breaking" a "strange poem, where sense is increasingly absent, where the enigmatic dominates, it tends to the dissolution of being, to the immense detachment that would have cleared the self and that would have ended the separation of the subject from the world" (*Œuvres complètes* 1368).

Sources:

Ashbery, John. "An Interview with Henri Michaux." *Reported Sightings. Art Chronicles 1957-1987.* New York: Alfred A. Knopf, 1989.

Jouffroy, Alain. "Henri Michaux: A Challenge to the Exterior World, Our Enemy of Today?" *Arts*, n. 726, June 20, 1959, p. 9.

Kuhn, Reinhard. "Prismatic Reflections: Michaux's Paix dans les brisements." *About French Poetry from Dada to Tel Quel.* Ed. Mary Ann Caws. Detroit: Wayne State University Press, 1974. p. 186-204.

Michaux, Henri. *Œuvres complètes II.* Ed. Raymond Bellour and Yse Tran. Paris: Editions Gallimard, 2001.

Michaux, Henri. *The Selected Writings of Henri Michaux.* Trans. Richard Ellman. New York: New Directions, 1990.

Michaux, Henri. *Tent Posts.* Trans. Lynn Hoggard. Los Angeles: Green Integer 4, 1977. First published as *Poteaux d'angle.* Paris: Editions Gallimard, 1983.

Michaux, Henri. *Miserable Miracle.* Trans. Louise Varese and Anna Moschovakis. Introduction by Octavio Paz. New York: New York Review Books Classics, 2002. First published as *Misérable miracle.* Paris: Éd. Du Rocher, 1956. (please cut Editions Gallimard, 1972).

Riguad-Drayton, Margaret. *Henri Michaux: Poetry, Painting, and the Universal Sign.* Oxford: Clarendon Press, Oxford University Press, 2005.

Schwabsky, Barry. "Henri Michaux,*"ArtForum*, May 1999.

THOUSAND TIMES BROKEN

Three Books

PAIX
DANS LES BRISEMENTS

PEACE
IN THE BREAKING

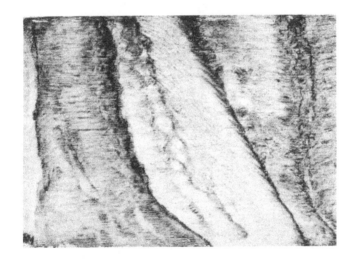

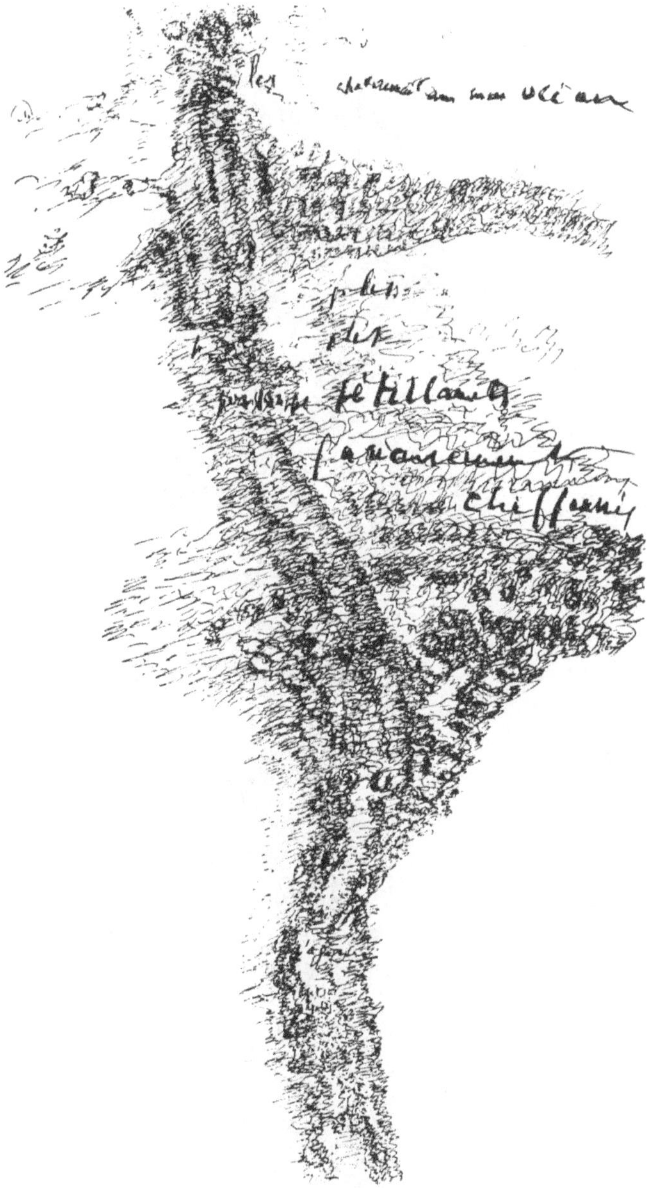
les
plis

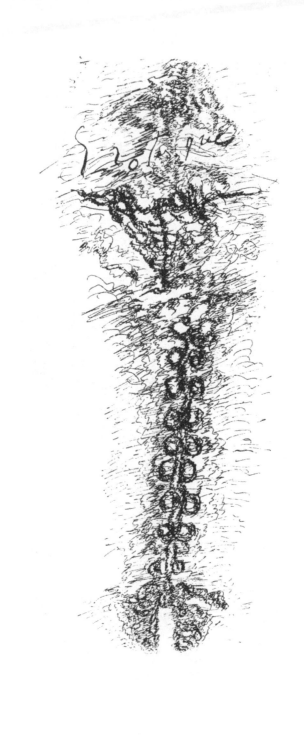

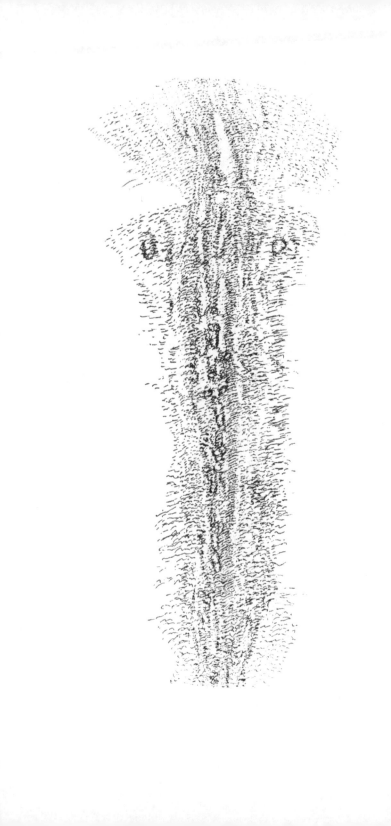

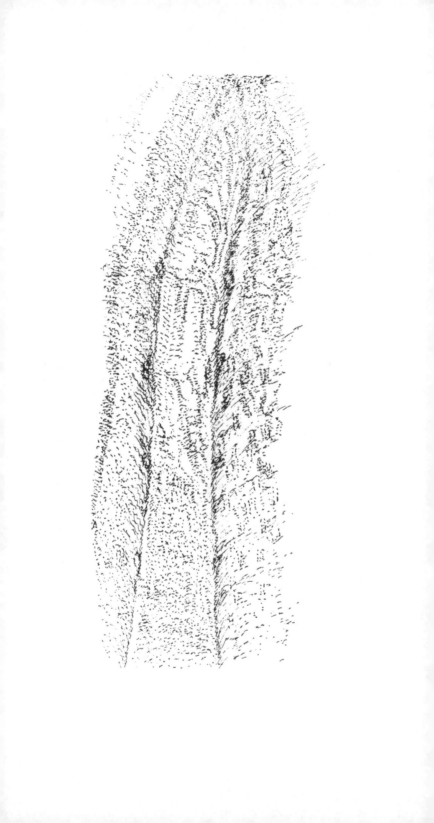

SIGNIFICATION DES DESSINS

Ça débouchait ainsi. Mais plus violemment, plus électriquement, plus fantastiquement.

Pendant des heures, les premières surtout, les plus porteuses d'images.

Les yeux fermés, visionnairement, je regardais se précipiter tumultueusement une sorte de torrent vertical. Par-dessus, des images, ou rien (quand je ne savais que penser de la confondante aventure), ou des mots par-ci, par-là, réflexions visualisées instantanément en lettres écrites ou même imprimées et qu'on n'entendait jamais. Car, avec des apparences qui pouvaient tromper, ces spectacles, c'était toujours des réflexions ou à propos de réflexions, qui, de temps à autre, me traversant l'esprit, amerrissaient sur ce torrent, qui paraissait être mon temps, mon temps devenu extraordinaire et que, devenu moi-même extraordinaire grâce à ce que j'avais pris,* j'arrivais à percevoir . . . et à imager.

Mon temps réellement ? Ou ma présence à ce temps ? Ma présence surexcitée, convergente ou parallèle, follement active, follement aux aguets, follement vigilante.

Plus profonde était la transe, et forte la dose avalée, plus grande était la vitesse d'apparition, de transformation, de succession du ruisselet phénoménal (peut-être d'ailleurs témoin d'un autre flux) car, pour couler, je ne jurerais pas qu'il fît.

---

* de la mescaline

MEANING OF THE DRAWINGS

That's how it came out. But more violently, more electrically, more fantastically.

For hours, especially during the first hours, the most promising in images.

With my eyes closed, like a visionary, I watched a sort of vertical torrent rush tumultuously. Over that, images, or nothing (when I couldn't think about anything other than the confounding adventure), or words here, there, reflections visualized instantly in letters written or even printed and that were never heard. Since, with appearances that could be misleading, these spectacles were always reflections or about reflections that, from time to time, went through my mind, splashing down on this torrent that seemed to be my time, my time that had become extraordinary and that, having become extraordinary myself thanks to what I had taken,* I had come to perceive . . . and imagine.

Was it really my time? Or my presence at that time? My overexcited, convergent, or parallel presence, madly active, madly alert, madly vigilant.

The deeper the trance, and the stronger the dose swallowed, the greater the speed at which the phenomenal rivulet appeared, transformed, running, (possibly also the witness of another flow) because I would not swear that it flowed.

---

* Mescaline.

Quoique la succession de vues différentes parût évidente, était-ce vraiment couler ? N'était-ce pas <<couler sans couler>>, autre absurdité, autre réalité stupéfiante ? N'était-ce pas substitution ininterrompue ?

Ce tapis vibratile, qui avait quelque chose de commun avec des décharges électriques à étincelles ramifiées, et aussi avec des spectres magnétiques, ce je ne sais quoi de tremblant, d'ardent, de fourmillant, semblable à des spasmes faits nerfs, cet arbre aux fines branches, qui pouvaient aussi bien être des éclatements latéraux, ce fluide tempétueux, contractile, secoué, champagnisé, mais élastiquement retenu et empêché de déborder par une sorte de tension superficielle, ce nerveux écran de projection, plus énigmatique encore que les visions qui s'y posaient, je ne sais, je ne saurai jamais en parler convenablement. On n'en connaît pas d'autre. On n'a pas, que je sache, entendu parler d'un semblable. Qui sait pourtant si un jour, par quelque nouvelle intervention sur les lieux de l'esprit, ne le verra pas, presque qui le voudra, et alors mon modèle, singulier jusqu'à présent, sera reconnu.

Cependant il bouillonnait, furieux, impétueux, devant moi, pour moi, à travers moi, moi aussi bouillonnant, éperdument penché sur l'en-avant, l'en-avant, l'en-avant, dans la précipitation, les rafales, les arrachements, penché, interdit surtout devant ces passages miens révélés sur le petit écran inattendu, incroyablement lumineux, dans un silence total, dans un silence déroutant.

Mon trouble était grand. La dévastation était plus grande. La vitesse plus grande encore. Dans un non sonore vrombissement, il y avait accentuation, il y avait augmentation, il y avait poussée, il y avait intensité, il y avait énormité, il y avait paroxysme, il y avait dislocation, il y avait surstimulation et, comme par l'effet de quantité de minuscules sabotages, il y avait désorganisation, avec toujours

Even though the succession of different views seemed obvious, was this really flowing? Wasn't this "flowing without flowing," another absurdity, another astounding reality? Wasn't this an uninterrupted substitution?

This vibratile carpet, which had something in common with electrical discharges with ramified sparks, as well as with magnetic spectra, a certain something that trembled, that burned, that tingled, like spasms turned into nerves, this tree with fine branches, that could also be lateral bursts, that tempestuous fluid, contractile, shaken, effervescent, but elastically held and kept from overflowing through some sort of surface tension, that nervous projection screen, even more enigmatic than the visions that arose on it, I don't know, I will never know how to talk about it properly. No other example is known of. As far as I know, no one has heard of anything similar. Yet who knows whether, one day, through some new intervention in the places of the mind, almost anyone who wants will see it, and then my model, unique until now, will be recognized.

Nevertheless it seethed, furious, impetuous, before me, for me, through me, while I seethed too, frantically intent on what moved forward, forward, forward, within the precipitation, the gusts, the wrenchings, intent, dumbfounded especially before those passages of mine revealed on the unexpected small screen, which was incredibly luminous, within a complete silence, within a bewildering silence.

My agitation was great. The devastation was greater. The speed even greater. Within an insonorous hum, there was accentuation, there was augmentation, there was thrust, there was intensity, there was enormity, there was paroxysm, there was dislocation, there was overstimulation and, as if through the effect of many minuscule sabotages, there was disorganization, however always with

cependant par-derrière une organisation surtendue, prête à péter, mais, en attendant, invraisemblablement actuelle et à son affaire, démonstration formidable de la prodigieuse vie du mental qui ne se peut arrêter.

J'avais sur ce qui se passait une saisie inouïe. Les moindres changements, les plus infimes matières à perception qui jamais autrement n'eussent en moi rencontré un grain de conscience, j'étais dessus à l'instant, d'un bond de tigre. Je me tenais devant, électriquement alerté, moi comme dédoublé, elles décuplées en netteté, en vitesse, en évidence. Je vivais intense dans la microperception, les microsignaux, avec des pensées express et des réflexions à l'état d'éclairs.

Dans la plus abstraite, tout à coup parfois un élément, rarement le plus important, accrochait en rappel une situation-souvenir ou plusieurs tableaux à la file comme en ricochet (c'était alors bien plus étonnant), ou bien une analogie faisait *image,* malgré moi et sans moi évoquée, se plaquait violente et colorée sur l'écran fluidique, ou bien, lors d'évocations en chaîne, à d'autres s'agglomérait en macles saugrenus, soudains coq-à-l'âne indéchiffrables, frappants et vides, non-sens ahurissants et usurpateurs.

Par la merveille de mon état exceptionnel, je percevais ce qu'autrement on ne perçoit pas, dont on se doute à peine, ou pas du tout. J'étais à cette fenêtre, je n'étais plus qu'à cette fenêtre, à ce drap vibrant, déchiré, claquant sans aucun bruit, où se déroulait un monde.

Fait digne d'une parenthèse, les Chinois, qui eurent pendant longtemps une inclination, un vrai génie de la modestie pour imiter la nature, suivre le sens, l'allure des phénomènes naturels et leur rester conjoints en sympathie par une sorte d'intelligence poétique, ont, a l'inverse de presque tous les autres peuples de cette terre, conçu

a very strained organization in the background, ready to burst, but, in the meantime, incredibly present and in its element, a formidable demonstration of the prodigious life of the mental state that could not stop.

I had an incredible grasp of what was happening. The slightest changes, the tiniest materials of perception which otherwise never would have aroused a flicker of consciousness in me, I was on them in an instant, like a tiger pouncing. I stood before them, electrically alert, as if split in two, and they were multiplying neatly, rapidly, manifestly. I was living intensely in the microperception, the microsignals, with express thoughts and lightning reflections.

In the most abstract, all of a sudden, sometimes an element, rarely the most important one, hung in abseil of a memory-situation or several pictures in a row as though ricocheting (this was thus much more astonishing), or rather an analogy became an *image,* despite me and without my evoking it, plastering itself violently and colorfully on the fluidic screen, or rather, during evocations in a series, with others that gathered in preposterous macles, suddenly talking indecipherable non-sequiturs, striking and empty, nonsense that astounds and usurps.

Through the wonder of my exceptional state, I perceived what one otherwise doesn't perceive, what one hardly suspects if at all. I was at that window, I was no longer anywhere but at that window, at that torn vibrating sheet, noiselessly snapping, where a world was unfolding.

A fact worthy of digression, the Chinese, who have had for a long time an inclination, a true genius of modesty for imitating nature, following the direction, the pace of natural phenomena and remaining joined in sympathy with them by some sort of poetic intelligence, have, conversely to nearly all other peoples on this Earth, conceived

et utilisé une écriture qui suit la pensée de haut en bas suiv-
ant son débouché naturel.*

Fait non moins curieux, les mots y sont des caractères,
fermes, fixes, signes qui sont avant tout à voir.**

Et peu ou pas de syntaxe. Rapports grammaticaux
souterrains, à deviner. L'exposé, chez eux, est surtout un
tableau, tableau fait de tableaux fixes, invariants. Proche en-
core de la pensée visionnaire, de l'apparition originelle du
phénomène premier de la pensée.*** Mais abandonnons cela.
Langues toutes tellement fortes, tellement possédantes.

Je parle ici d'autre chose. Je parle du débouché éruptif,
incoercible des pensées lorsqu'on se trouve dans l'état in-
comparable à tout autre.

Alors que chez un homme de n'importe quelle culture
dans son état normal, les pensées qui lui apparaissent ne
vont pas en rester là, sont lentes ou qu'il va ralentir, mais
qu'avant tout il va examiner, discuter, juger, structurer, édi-
fier, véritables macropensées de synthèse, sur lesquelles il
va avoir action, *l'action de la volonté* qui va les diriger, les
rattacher, les grouper, les essayer, les mettre de côté pour
plus tard se les remémorer, les combiner, inlassablement
les combiner, les organiser, les subordonner, *l'action* (non
moins importante, non moins faite d'énergie, non moins
directrice) qui part *du gout de jouer*, de s'en amuser, de les
parer, de faire des gammes, des variations, des soi-disantes

---

* Si le naturel est ce qui m'a paru tel.
** Dont les prononciations d'un lieu à un autre peuvent varier du tout au tout.
*** Toutes différentes sont les autres langues, qui ont évolué loin du donné
primitif, maintenant caché, pour s'adonner au discours et à ce qui lui est
le plus utile, à tout ce qui, par variations des composants, par conjugaisons
et déclinaisons complexes, suffixes, etc., permet de plus précises interrela-
tions et interdéterminations, et de façon générale répond au besoin de faire
la police d'une circulation sévèrement dirigée. Langues de la contrainte.
Conrainte et volonté. Chinois, moins de contrainte. Mescaline, plus aucune
contrainte. Plus de rapports grammaticaux non plus.

and used a type of writing that follows thought from top to bottom along its natural outlet.*

A fact no less curious, words there are of characters, firm, fixed signs that are above all made to be seen.**

And little or no syntax. Subterranean grammatical connections, to be guessed at. What their words present above all is a picture, a picture made of fixed, invariant pictures. Still close to visionary thought, the original appearance of the first phenomenon of thought.*** But let's abandon this. Languages all so strong, so possessing.

I'm talking about something else here. I am talking about the eruptive, irrepressible emergence of thoughts when one is in the state comparable to no other.

Whereas in a man of any culture in his normal state, the thoughts that appear to him will not remain as such; they are slow or he will slow them down, but, above all he will examine, discuss, judge, structure, construct real macrothoughts of synthesis, over which there will be an action, *the action of the will* that will direct them, bind them, group them, try them, put them aside for later to remember, combine them, tirelessly combine them, organize them, subordinate them, *the action* (no less important, no less made of energy, no less directive) that stems *from the taste for playing,* to enjoy them, to adorn them, to play scales, variations, so-called

* If the natural is what seemed to me as such.
** And whose pronunciation may be completely different from one place to another.
*** The other languages are all different, having evolved far from the primitive given, now hidden, in order to devote itself to speech and to what is most useful to it, to everything that, through variations of components, through complex conjugations and declensions, suffixes, etc., allows more precise interrelationships and inter-determinations, and in a general way responds to the need of policing severely directed traffic. Languages of constraint. Constraint and will. Chinese, fewer constraints. Mescaline, no more constraints. No more grammatical connections either.

improvisations (!) ou simplement *l'action* qui vient du désir d' *intervenir*, d'établi des vérités, des contre-vérités, des mensonges, de gâcher, d'*inventer*, d'ordonner, de désordonner, de diversifier, etc. Les pensées, au contraire, que l'on rencontre dans la transe mescalinienne ont une allure toute différente.

Vite elles viennent, vite, vite, follement vite à la file indienne, passent, fuient, disparaissent, pensées a l'état naissant, pensées en liberté, les seules que l'on connaisse libres[*] (avec du reste tous ses inconvénients), sur lesquelles vous, ni vos désirs, ni votre volonté ne pourrez rien, ni pour les trier, ni pour quoi que ce soit.

Pensées parcellaires et qui le resteront, individuelles, ingouvernables, inutilisables, intraitables, impermanentes, apparitionnelles, aussitôt perdues qu'apparues, ne subsistant pas, ne préparant à rien, impossibles à piloter,[**] à reprendre, à placer autrement, à retrouver, à rêver dessus, impossibles à noter dans leur sauvage éjection, méchantes parfois, mais innocentes toujours, jamais stratèges, impudentes, mais incroyablement éblouissantes, clarifiantes, pensées qui passent dans un presque néant syntaxique, dont on se passe fort bien . . . tant qu'on n'essaie pas d'écrire.

Mes dessins expriment l'épiphénomène se produisant irrégulièrement au passage de telle ou telle réflexion.

Ce sont—images ou mots—les dépôts instantanés, occasionnels, (fugitifs, mais indéplaçables sur le moment, fixes et comme invisiblement fléchés sur place), provoqués par les évocations involontaires et qui toujours surprennent, et que j'appellerais bien des <<laisses de réflexion>>.

---

[*] Car les rêveries, c'est toujours dirigé, peu ou prou. Quant aux rêves, la pensée y est communément impure, dissimulée, non abstraite, obligée de se manifester en tableaux, en théâtre, en épisodes et plutôt mal que bien.
[**] Activité mentale bientôt totalement inefficace, qui si elle dure, deviendra celle de la manie et du délire.

improvisations (!) or simply *the action* that stems from the desire to *intervene,* to establish truths, countertruths, lies, to ruin, to *invent,* to order, to disorder, to diversify, etc. Thoughts, on the contrary, that one finds in the mescaline trance have a completely different pace.

Fast, they come fast, fast in single file, passing, fleeing, disappearing, thoughts in a nascent state, thoughts in freedom, the only ones known to be free* (with moreover all the inconveniences), about which neither you, nor your desires, nor your will can do anything, neither to sort them out nor to do anything else.

Fragmented thoughts that will remain so, individual, ungovernable, unusable, intractable, impermanent, apparitional, lost as quickly as they appear, not remaining, not preparing anything, impossible to direct,** to resume, to place otherwise, to find again, to dream over, impossible to note within their wild ejection, sometimes malicious, but always innocent, never strategists, impudent, but incredibly dazzling, clarifying, thoughts that pass into a syntactical nothingness, which one does very well without . . . as long as one does not attempt to write.

My drawings express the epiphenomenon occurring irregularly in the passage of this or that reflection.

They are—images or words—instantaneous, occasional deposits (fugitive but unmovable, fixed and as if invisibly marked out by arrows on the spot), provoked by the involuntary evocations that always surprise, which I would call "leashes of reflection."

---

* Because reveries are always more or less directed. As for dreams, thought there is often impure, concealed, not abstract, forced to manifest itself as pictures, as theater, as episodes, and more often badly than well.
** A mental activity soon completely ineffective and which, if it lasts, will become that of mania and delirium.

Je n'en donne que peu de pages. Plus serait fastidieux, mènerait à d'autres commentaires qui n'ont que faire ici, à expliquer des visions, lambeaux d'histoires personnelles à n'en plus finir, chaînons de la chaîne excessivement longue des associations.

Malgré son air curieux, original, je crois montrer un phénomène de base, qui devait être découvert un jour. Ici éclatant et nu, exceptionnel dans un état exceptionnel, mais qui—ou je me trompe fort—est primitif et général, sous-jacent chez l'homme même le plus placide à l'intelligence la plus dirigée, la plus volontaire, et qui, peut-être vaguement éprouvé, mais non vu, passe inaperçu derrière d'autres perceptions qui intéressent davantage.

Je crois donc montrer, ayant plusieurs fois pendant des heures été en sa présence alors prodigieuse, je crois montrer l'arbre sans fin, l'arbre de vie qui est une source, qui est, piqueté d'images et de mots et proposant des énigmes, l'écoulement, qui, sans interruption, même d'une seule seconde, traverse l'homme du premier instant de sa vie au tout dernier, ruisseau ou sablier qui ne s'arrête qu'avec elle.

Un rouleau, un kakémono l'aurait rendu mieux qu'un livre, à condition de pouvoir se dérouler, ou un volume a page unique indéfiniment dépliée.

Les présents dessins—dois-je le dire ?—sont des reconstitutions. Une main deux cents fois plus agile que la main humaine, ne suffirait pas à la tâche de suivre la course accélérée du spectacle intarissable.

Et pas question de faire autre chose que de suivre. On ne peut ici s'emparer d'une pensée, d'un terme, d'une figure, pour les travailler, s'en inspirer, improviser dessus. Tout pouvoir perdu sur eux. Leur vitesse, leur indépendance est à ce prix.

I am providing only a few pages of them. More would be tedious, leading to other comments that have no place here, to explain visions, scraps of interminable personal stories, links in the excessively long chain of associations.

Despite their interesting, original appearance, I believe I am indicating a basic phenomenon, which had to be discovered one day. Here, dazzling and bare, exceptional in an exceptional state, but which—unless I am very much mistaken—is primitive and general, underlying in even the most placid man, with the most directed and willful intelligence, and which, perhaps vaguely experienced but not seen, goes unnoticed behind other perceptions that are more interesting.

Thus I believe I am indicating, having spent hours in its then-prodigious presence several times, I believe I am indicating the endless tree, the tree of life that is a source, that is, dotted with images and words and proposing enigmas, the flow that, without interruption, even for a single second, passes through man from the first moment of his life to the very last one, a stream or an hourglass that stops only when life stops.

A scroll, a kakemono would have rendered that flow better than a book, as long as it could unroll, or else a volume of a single page that unfolds forever.

These drawings—must I say it?—are reconstructions. A hand two hundred times more agile than the human hand would not suffice for the task of following the accelerated course of the inexhaustible spectacle.

And it is out of the question to do more than follow. Here one cannot seize a thought, a term, or a figure, to work with it, to draw inspirations from it, or to improvise on it. All power over them is lost. Their speed, their independence, comes at that price.

AU SUJET DE
PAIX DANS LES BRISEMENTS

Je n'ai pas, dans cet écrit, suivi ou tenté de suivre la dégringolade, la précipitation, l'accélération des apparitions, des visions, des impressions, des impulsions, des pensées.

Je l'ai montrée ailleurs* maintes fois. Nous n'avons plus les mêmes rapports, la mescaline et moi. En tout ce qui est répété, quelque chose s'épuise et quelque chose mûrit. Une sorte de plus profond équilibre est obscurément cherché et partiellement trouvé.

À des centaines de vagues qui frappent sa coque, le navire répond par un ample mouvement de tangage. Sous les coups, on tend à retrouver une unité. Appui sur eux. Sustentation. Les ondes, qui font dislocation, peuvent être aussi rayonnement.

Le poème mille fois brisé pèse et pousse pour se constituer, pour un immense jour mémorable reconstituer, pour, à travers tout, nous reconstituer.

---

* *Misérable miracle,* Monaco, Éd. du Rocher, 1956. *L'Infini turbulent,* Éd. Mercure de France, 1957.

ON THE SUBJECT OF
PEACE IN THE BREAKING

I have not, in this writing, followed or attempted to follow the tumbling down, the haste, the acceleration of the appearances, the visions, the impressions, the impulses, the thoughts.

I have done that elsewhere* many times. We don't have the same relationship, mescaline and I. In everything that is repeated, something exhausts itself and something else ripens. A sort of deeper balance is dimly sought and partially found.

To the hundreds of waves striking its hull, the ship responds by ample pitching motions. Under the blows, we seem to regain a unity. Rely on them. Sustenance. The waves, which break things up, can also be radiant.

The poem, a thousand times broken, presses and pushes to construct itself, to reconstruct, for one immense unforgettable day, in order to, through everything, reconstruct us.

---

* *Misérable miracle,* Monaco, Éd. Du Rocher, 1956. *L'Infini turbulent,* Éd. Mercure de France, 1957.
English editions: *Miserable Miracle*, San Francisco, City Lights, 1963, translated by Louise Varèse. *Miserable Miracle*, New York, New York Review Books Classics, 2002, translated by Louise Varèse, addenda Anna Moschovakis. *The Infinite Turbulence*, London, Calder & Boyars, 1975, translated by Michael Fineberg.

PAIX DANS LES BRISEMENTS

l'espace a toussé sur moi
et voilà que je ne suis plus
les cieux roulent des yeux
des yeux qui ne disent rien et ne savent pas grand-chose

de mille écrasements écrasé
allongé à l'infini
témoin d'infini
infini tout de même
mis à l'infini

patrie qui se propose
qui n'emploie pas mes deux mains
mais me broie mille mains
que je reconnais et pourtant ne connaissais
qui m'embrasse et par brassage
à moi me soustrait, m'ouvre et m'assimile

à l'essaim je retourne
des milliers d'ailes d'hirondelles tremblent sur ma vie

prisme
dans le prisme je me pose, j'ai séjour

temps de la solennité

PEACE IN THE BREAKING

space coughed up on me
and then I no longer exist
the skies roll their eyes
the eyes that say nothing and don't know much

from a thousand crushings crushed
extended to infinity
witness of infinity
infinite all the same
set to infinity

native land that offers
that doesn't use my two hands
but that grinds up a thousand hands
that I recognize yet do not know
that embraces me and through mixing
subtracts me from myself, opens me up, and assimilates me

to the swarm I return
thousands of swallows' wings tremble across my life

prism
I settle into the prism, I dwell there

time of solemnity

je reçois les ondes qui donnent indifférence
impure et précaire la petite vie s'éloigne de la Vie
poussée des fantômes contre moi

sillon
la forme fendue d'un être immense
m'accompagne et m'est sœur
j'écoute les milliers de feuilles

l'impression suraiguë du malaise de moi
accompagne l'impression suraiguë de l'aise de moi
de l'aise vertigineuse
de l'aise à son extrême

un désir d'union
oh ce désir d'union

fluide, fertile
double du double
double de tout redoublement

pétales ouverts
pétales sans fin, parfumés du parfum de l'indicible
la fleur du perpétuel

fontaines
le pouls de la fenêtre s'éveille
le pouls lumineux du point du jour
éblouissant
éblouissant

tir dans la tête
feu silencieux des photons

I receive the waves that bring indifference
impure and precarious the small life withdraws from the Life
pushed by ghosts against me

furrow
the split form of an immense being
accompanies me and is my sister
I listen to the thousands of leaves

the overly acute impression of my displeasure
accompanies the overly acute impression of my pleasure
of the vertiginous pleasure
of pleasure at its most extreme

a desire for union
oh that desire for union

fluid, fertile
double of the double
double of any redoubling

open petals
petals without an end, perfumed with the perfume of the unsayable
the flower of the perpetual

fountains
the pulse of the window awakens
the luminous pulse of the break of day
dazzling
dazzling

shot in the head
silent fire of photons

foudres blanches
foudres prolongées
foudres sans arrêt

frissons
immense environnement

rafales
rafales violettes
rafales sur l'oiseau

en un haut espace sous mon front ouvert
soudain
je vois

s'étageant
s'étageant
s'étageant à l'infini
angulairement
angulairement
angulairement
d'énormes, de gigantesques flamboyants
monuments gothiques
fusants, exaspérés, énergumènes
à accélération,
à élancements gothiques
à gammes gothiques
à balistique gothique
jet-gotic . . .

gêne
cristaux maintenant et colonnettes

ridicule!

white lightning
prolonged lightning
endless lightning

chills
immense environs

gusts
violet gusts
gusts against the bird

in a high space under my open forehead
suddenly
I see

rising themselves in tiers
rising themselves
rising themselves to infinity
angularly
angularly
angularly
enormous, giant, flamboyant
Gothic monuments
fusing, exasperated, maniacs
of acceleration,
of Gothic stabs
of Gothic scales
of Gothic ballistics
Gothic jet . . .

discomfort
crystals now and slender little columns

ridiculous!

portiques, pavillons
pédonculés
fluets
fins
filants
ajourés
petits
pointus
minarettants
. . . .

honte, oh cette lascivité dans les couleurs!
froissements optiques de la perverse caresse de la scintillation
vues maculatrices à chaque instant crachées sur moi

c'est ignoble d'avoir vécu

foulé par toute cette foule
que de foules!
la foule qui refoule l'ange

dans l'âme tétanisée, tout ce qui passe!
monŝtruellement . . .
l'être épuisé, mais géniteur, d'autant plus géniteur
géniteur sans le savoir
la torsion des lignes: signe des vices

je sais maintenant
je sais

la ligne qui pervertit,
qui entraîne
et le baroque . . .

je sais

porticos, pavilions
pedunculate
slender
fine
flowing
openwork
small
pointy
like minarets

. . . .

shame, oh that lasciviousness in the colors!
optical creasings of the perverse caress of scintillation
at every moment spat on by macular sights

to have lived is ignoble

trampled by this whole crowd
nothing but crowds!
crowd that repulses the angel

all that goes on in the tetanized soul!
monstrously . . .
the exhausted being, but a genitor, all the more a genitor
a genitor without knowing it
the twist of the lines: sign of vices

I know now
I know

the line that perverts
that drags you along
and the baroque . . .

I know

cependant l'espace et l'espace mien qui me démange
continuellement bougeons et bouillonnons

ocelles
infini d'ocelles qui pullule
je me prête aux ocelles
aux infimes déchirures, aux volutes
je me plie aux mille plis qui me plient, me déplient
petits traîtres qui vertigineusement m'effilochent
je laisse en frissonnant tirer les sonnettes sans fin
qui sans cesse pour rien m'appellent

infini
infini qui au corps me travaille
et rit de mon fini
qui en frémissements éludants et par retraits
fait poussière de mon fini
infini qui m'étend
et sans effort, sans spectacle
de mes prises me dessaisit

Blanche vermine de broderies trop fines
qui court partout et ne se rend nulle part,
trop fine, trop fine
et m'étire,
me mine
et m'effile

espace
qui en dentelles éperdument m'horripile
me crible
et l'esprit m'épile

however the space and my space that itches
let's continuously move and bubble

ocelli
infinite ocelli that swarm
I lend myself to the ocelli
to the infirm rips, to the volutes
I fold myself in a thousand folds that fold me, unfold me
small traitors that vertiginously fray me
I shiver allowing the pulling of never-ending bells
that call me incessantly for nothing

infinity
infinity that torments my body
and that laughs at my finish
and that in elusive shudders and through retreats
turns my finish into dust
infinity that extends me
and without effort, without spectacle
relinquishes me from my holds

White vermin with overly fine embroidery
that runs everywhere and gets nowhere
too fine, too fine
and that stretches me
undermines me
and frays me

space
that madly horripilates me in lace
riddles me
and plucks out my mind

foule
folle foule fuselée
frissons traduits en palais ciselés
aux colonnettes trop sveltes, trop sveltes

brillance par défaillance
ornements par chatouillement
stalactites par glissements
en vérité de la poudre que j'ai mangée
sont sortis tous ces plis
ces plis et tout ce qui luit
et tout ce qui se contredit et me contredit
et dit contre ce que je dis quand je dis que je . . .
miettes de je
miettes au loin de <<j . . .>>

de grands <<S>> obliques
m'obligent à serpentiner
difficultés recourbées

le multiple me dépèce
malmené
down
pf
pf
pf
des empêche-pensées
sans cesse subitement me subtilisent
tenant ma tête sous foisonnement
intolabel
intolabel
intolabel

je lutte
atroce
atroce, le torrentiel

crowd
crazed crookback crowd
chills translated into chiseled palaces
with columns that are too slender, too slender

brilliance through failure
ornaments through tickling
stalactites through sliding
in fact because of the powder I have eaten
all those creases have come out
those creases and all that gleams
and all that contradicts itself and contradicts me
and contradicts what I say when I say that I . . .
crumbs of I
crumbs far away from "I . . ."

big oblique *S*'s
force me to serpent
curved difficulties

the multiple cuts me up
manhandled
down
pf
pf
pf
thought stoppers
incessantly suddenly whisk me away
keeping my head under expansion
intolabel
intolabel
intolabel

I fight
atrocious
atrocious, the torrential

se souvenir
il faudra se souvenir

traversé de troupeaux de paroxysmes
vingt mille cascades coulent en moi

l'enfer devient laine
transport
une âme immense veut entrer dans mon âme
des îles incessamment chavirent dans mon océan

passages
passages à plis
passages pétillants
passages furieusement chiffonnés

totalement à bas
mâché

on me lape
j'agonise
j'aime, j'épouse ma mort

dipht
dipht
dipht

je coule
on me laisse remourir enore

je coule
sable du sablier de mon temps
précipitamment s'effondrant
précipitamment
comme torrents de montagne
jusques à quand ?

remembering
remembering will be necessary

crossed by herds of paroxysms
twenty thousand cascades flow through me

hell becomes wool
transport
an immense soul wants to enter my soul
islands incessantly capsize in my ocean

passages
passages with folds
sparkling passages
furiously rumpled passages

totally low
chewed

I'm lapped up
I lie dying
I love, I marry my death

dipht
dipht
dipht

I flow
I am allowed to die again again

I flow
sand in the hourglass of my time
precipitously collapsing
precipitously
like mountain torrents
until when?

une grande séquence d'envolées
d'envolées à vide, abstraites
d'envolées-ah

l'enthousiasme est un composé,
ici ses successifs déclics, particules d'élans . . .

oh risible ! oh misérable !
sans cesse
tchit
tchit

pirates soudains
sans cesse

il naît
il naît des commencements
trop
trop
trop vite
qui se répètent
et incessamment répètent que je répète que <<ça se répète>>
et que je répète que je répète que je répète que <<ça se répète>>
écho de l'écho de l'écho jamais éteint

trop
trop secoué pour dire
ne puis

présences multiples
enlace . . . entrelace . . . ce qui entrelace . . .
l'infini est serpent

cependant, le manteau de lumière, là, presque . . . bientôt

a great sequence of flights
of empty flights, abstract
flights-ah

enthusiasm is a compound,
here successive clicks, particles of momentum . . .

oh laughable! oh miserable!
incessant
tchit
tchit

suddenly pirates
incessant

it is born
it is born from beginnings
too
too
too fast
that repeat
and incessantly repeat that I repeat "it repeats"
and that I repeat that I repeat that I repeat "it repeats"
echo of the echo of the echo without end

too
too shaken to tell
can neither

multiple presences
interlace . . . intertwine . . . that which intertwines . . .
infinity is a snake

however, the mantle of light, there, almost . . . soon

une force
une force d'agrandissement heureux
effarante extension
une force jusqu'au bout du monde
comment calmer les ailes innombrables de la force qui
m'élève
qui m'élève de plus en plus ?

paix
paix par graine broyée
je fais la paix

dans une douceur de soie
m'élevant sans privilèges
tous les feuillages des forêts de la terre ont le frémissement
à l'unisson duquel je frissonne

un étrange allongement
un étrange prolongement
un dénuement surabondant
une continue lévitation
pourrai-je jamais redescendre ?

sauf !

j'ai brisé la coquille
simple je sors du carcel de mon corps
l'air
l'au-delà de l'air est mon protecteur

l'inondation a soulevé mes fardeaux
l'abandon de l'empire de moi m'a étendu infiniment
plus n'ai besoin de mon cadavre
je ne vis plus que de la vie du temple

dans la région du primordial, le récitant se tait

a force
a force of joyful growth
staggering extension
a force going to the end of the world
how to calm the countless wings of the force that
lifts me
lifts me more and more?

peace
peace through crushed seeds
I make peace

with the softness of silk
raising me up without privileges
all the foliage of the forests of the Earth has the shuddering
in whose unison I shudder

a strange lengthening
a strange prolongation
a superabundant destitution
a continuous levitation
will I ever be able to descend again?

except!

I have broken my shell
simple I leave the prison of my body
the air
the beyond of the air is my protector

the flood has lifted my burdens
the abandonment of the empire of myself has extended me infinitely
no need now of my corpse
the only life I lead is the life of the temple

in the region of the primordial, the narrator shuts up

celui qui est ici n'est plus revêtu
hors de son corps le désert l'approvisionne

le mal est immolé au bien
l'impur au pur
l'à-côté au droit
le nombre à l'unique
et le nom est immolé au sans nom

pureté m'enfante
j'ai passé la porte
je passe une nouvelle porte
sans bouger, je passe de nouvelles portes

l'eau qui m'enlève, plus légère que les eaux de la terre
enlève aussi les nuages épais du firmament de mon âme

tremblement si petit en moi
qui m'entretient une si grande paix . . .

objet n'est plus obstacle
savoir, calcul n'est plus obstacle
mémoire n'est plus obstacle

j'ai laissé derrière moi le sot, le sûr, le compétiteur

à cause d'extrême minceur je passe
à cause d'une minceur qui dans la nature n'a pas d'égale
le courant léger, omnipotent m'a dépouillé
mes déchets ne collent plus à moi
je n'ai plus de déchets

purifié des masses
purifié des densités
tous rapports purifiés dans le miroir des miroirs

the one who is here is no longer covered
outside his body the desert provides for him

evil is sacrificed to the good
the impure to the pure
the nearby to the straight ahead
the number to the unique
and the name is sacrificed to the nameless

purity gives birth to me
I have gone through the door
I go through a new door
without moving, I go through new doors

the water that pulls me away, lighter than the waters of the Earth
also pulls away the thick clouds of the firmament of my soul

trembling so small in me
that preserves for me such a great peace . . .

objects are no longer obstacles
knowing, calculation are no longer obstacles
memory is no longer an obstacle

I leave behind the fool, the certain, the competitor

because of my extreme thinness I pass through
because of a thinness that has no equal in nature
the light omnipotent current has stripped me
my waste no longer sticks to me
I have no more waste

purified of masses
purified of densities
all connections purified in the mirror of mirrors

éclairé par ce qui m'éteint
porté par ce qui me noie
je suis fleuve dans le fleuve qui passe

que la tentation ne me vienne plus de m'arrêter
de me fixer de me situer
que la tentation ne me vienne plus d'interférer

bienheureuses ondes d'égalisation
qui d'une arche solennelle surmontent chaque instant
ondes qui donnent diadème et plaie

une souffrance presque exquise
traverse mon cœur dans ma poitrine

liée au ciment aimant qui tient le monde fraternel
indivisé et proche jusqu'en son plus lointain
et tout enclose dans le sanctuaire

cependant qu'un froid extrême
saisit les membres de mon corps déserté
mon âme déchargée de la charge de moi
suit dans un infini qui l'anime et ne se précise pas
la pente vers le haut
vers le haut
vers toujours plus haut
la pente
comment ne l'avais-je pas encore rencontrée?
la pente qui aspire
la merveilleusement simple inarrêtable ascension

illuminated by what extinguishes me
carried by what drowns me
I am a river in the passing river

may temptation come no more to stop me
to fixate me to situate me
may temptation come no more to interfere

blessed be the waves of equalization
that from a solemn arch overcome each instant
waves that bring diadem and wound

an almost exquisite suffering
goes through my heart in my chest

linked to the loving cement that holds the fraternal world
undivided and near till its most distant point
and all enclosed in the sanctuary

meanwhile an extreme cold
seizes the members of my deserted body
my soul unburdened of the burden of myself
follows in an infinity that animates it and does not take shape
the upward slope
upward
always farther upward
the slope
how had I not encountered it before?
the slope that aspires
the marvelously simple unstoppable ascent

VIGIES SUR CIBLES

1959

WATCHTOWERS ON TARGETS

1959

AFFAIRES IMPERSONNELLES

En se réveillant, il sentit un petit ventre dans la paume de sa main. De qui le ventre? Il ne voulut pas déranger. D'abord réfléchir. En réfléchissant, il se rendormit. Quand il se réveilla, plus de ventre. Plus personne.

Voilà, pris sur le fait, un des multiples inconvénients de la réflexion.

Autour de la retraite violée, il y eut presse. Tous voulaient assister à l'apoplexie du cygne.

Qu'il serait triste, empli de rage, de glaires, de faiblesse, d'étouffer, corps tordu, dans le fond d'une cucurbite.

Dans le blanc du cri, le crime s'est trahi, s'est jeté, épouvantable dans la conscience de tous les vivants présents dans les alentours. Il a fallu ouvrir les volets, les yeux et le reste languissant de la journée presque finie. Le criminel lui-même, transpercé par le cri, s'arrête et reste sans un mouvement. Le liquide rouge à l'infime balbutiement, appelé <<sang>>, ailleurs blut, ou blood, et même fièrement sangre, la lame du couteau, les traces et les empreintes de doigts vont bientôt témoigner contre celui qui maintenant

IMPERSONAL AFFAIRS

Waking up, he felt a small belly in the palm of his hand. Whose belly? He didn't want to disturb it. Reflect first. While reflecting, he fell asleep again. When he woke up, no more belly. No more anyone.

There, as a prime example, one of the many disadvantages of reflection.

Around the violated shelter, there was hurried activity. Everyone wanted to attend the apoplexy of the swan.

How sad it would be, filled with rage, with phlegm, with weakness, to suffocate, a twisted body, in the bottom of a gourd.

In the white of the cry, the crime betrayed itself, threw itself, terrible in the consciousness of all those living in the neighborhood. It was necessary to open the shutters, the eyes and the languishing rest of the almost finished day. The criminal himself, pierced by the cry, stops and does not make a move. The red liquid with the minute stammering, called "blood," elsewhere *blut,* or *blood,* and even proudly *sangre,* the blade of the knife, the marks and the fingerprints will soon testify against he who now flees, but

s'enfuit, mais en qui, immobile, verticale cathédrale en un instant érigée, le cri inattendu demeure et ne retombe pas.

☆

Venues de la forêt, apparaissent au printemps les larves volantes. Grandes, plus grandes que les plus grands oiseaux, et nombreuses, elles obscurcissent le ciel, elles obscurcissent les campagnes et les villages, blottis au creux des vallons, et qui voudraient se blottir davantage.

Le dénombrement des monstres se fait une fois l'an ou toutes les neuf lunes. Le sort est appelé à décider. Beaucoup périssent, mais assez survivent pour que monstrueusement se développent à nouveau les monstres des Haw.

☆

La mouche est si bien organisée qu'elle a pu fréquenter assidûment l'homme depuis des milliers d'années, sans être mise à la porte, ni mise à travailler. Le tout sans se gêner et ne cherchant nullement comme le chat à feindre d'être apprivoisée. Allant même jusqu'à s'installer au bord de ses yeux et à puiser jusque dans ses larmes admirablement salées l'appoint chlorure qui manque à son régime. Avec la même aisance elle fréquente aussi de plus gros mammifères aux yeux confortables et nul doute qu'elle ne rêve d'yeux plus parfaits encore c'est-à-dire comme des soucoupes, creusés au lieu de bombés.

Voilà l'être que tout homme en époque esclavagiste se doit de bien étudier au lieu des aigles, des lions, des chevaux ou des . . . maréchaux qui ne lui apprendront jamais ce qui tant importe: <<Comment cohabiter sans servir?>>

in whom, motionless, a vertical cathedral erected in one moment, the unexpected cry dwells and does not fade.

Coming from the forest, the flying larvae appear in spring. Large, larger than the largest birds, and in great numbers, they darken the sky, they darken the countryside and the villages, nestling together in the hollow of the small valleys, and wanting to nestle even more.

The counting of the monsters occurs once a year or every ninth moon. Fate is called to decide. Many perish, but enough survive so that the Haw monsters can monstrously gather again.

The fly is so well organized that it has been able to frequent man diligently for thousands of years, without being kicked out, or put to work. It has done all of this without interfering and without looking around stupidly like a cat pretending to be tamed. Going as far as to settle itself on the rim of one's eyes and drawing out from the admirably salted tears the exact chloride missing from its diet. With the same ease it frequents the comforts of the biggest mammals' eyes, no doubt dreaming of more perfect eyes yet, like saucers, sunken in rather than bulging out.

Here is the creature that every man should have studied in the slave era, instead of eagles, lions, horses or . . . marshals who will never teach him what is most important: "How to live together without serving?"

<<Moi aussi, dit Varisi, j'aurais besoin de souverainement traverser les pays et les espaces, ou au moins de monumentalement m'y installer. Mais je n'ai pas le port et la hauteur de l'arbre, je n'ai pas le royal et le concentre du tigre, je n'ai pas la masse et la majesté de la montagne.

<<Quelle a été la raison de ce triple manqué dans mon organisme, je me le demande.>>

Télépathie d'un astre à l'autre. C'est sur une autre planète que le Christ aurait été crucifié! Ah! Ah! voilà peut-être ce qui rendrait compte de ce qui paraissait si faux, si vrai, si faux . . .

"Me too, said Varisi, I would need sovereignty to cross countries and places, or at least to significantly settle there. But I do not have the bearing and height of the tree, I do not have the royalty and concentration of the tiger, I do not have the mass and the majesty of the mountain.

"What was the reason for this triple lack in my organism, I ask myself."

Telepathy from one star to another. It's on another planet that Christ would have been crucified! Ah! Ah! This would perhaps account for that which seemed so false, so true, so false . . .

Par les cheveux de l'âme, il la tenait pendant qu'elle agitait en elle-même de vains projets de résistance, qu'elle se débattait en vains mouvements, en vains retours, en vains délacements, glissant malgré elle, glissant déjà presque tout entière suspendue, sans appui, au-dessus de la fosse du désir partagé.

Il y a en moi, dit Raha, un mouvement vermiculaire. Je dirais des sottises en voulant mieux le situer et ne le toucherais pas davantage. Beaucoup d'autres mouvements, il est encore en moi, qui me retiennent loin de l'action, loin de l'attention qu'on attend de moi, et dont jamais je n'ai pu me désenivrer. Ignorants, qui s'obstinent à m'inviter. Ils ne savant pas. Raha doit se terrer. Comment voudrait-il se déterrer? . . . J'ai mes frontières près du centre. Il faut que je fasse vite, très vite, pour placer mon assurance. L'instant d'après je suis à l'étranger. Mais je sais, je sais à l'avance et me conduis conformément à sa géographie.

Savoir sa géographie, dit Raha . . .

By the hair of the soul, he held it while she waved herself in vain attempts of resistance, while she struggled in vain movements, in vain returns, in vain unlacings, slipping despite of it all, slipping almost entirely suspended, with no support above the pit of shared desire.

There is in me, Raha said, a wormlike movement. I would utter stupidities in wanting to situate it better and not touch it more. Many other movements, it's still in me, holding me far from the action, far from the attention expected of me, and from which I could never become sober. Idiots who insist on inviting me. They do not know. Raha must be underground. How would he want to dig? . . . I have my borders near the center. I have to be quick, very quick, to ensure my confidence. One minute later and I'm abroad. But I know, I know in advance and guide myself according to its geography.

Know its geography, Raha said . . .

<<Le miroir de l'âme, dit Agrigibi, me renvoie tantôt un chien, tantôt un crabe, tantôt une fourmi, tantôt une araignée, tantôt une belette prise dans un piège, tantôt un jeune hérisson aux piquants souples, tantôt un moustique blessé les ailes arrachées, en somme ma volonté moquée, défiate comme un billet froissé dans un bas de putain.>>

L'être dentelé, qui alors va parler en son nom?

Combien de fois Agrigibi ne rencontre-t-il pas des êtres de cyclone! Étrange? Non pas. C'est avec un continuel tonnerre de triomphe qu'avance partout le bien portant, frère du lion et du rouleau compresseur. Il jette avec force par sa peau, par ses yeux, un carrousel de fourches, pour forcer, pour percer, pour briser les endroits faibles des fragilement établis en eux-mêmes, lesquels ne peuvent faire fléchir le mécanisme de la bourrasque qui se croit homme et lui n'est que tournoiement, que tourbillon, qu'écrasement, que persécution, que déflagration, que menace incessante de déflagration.

Comment résister?

Comment avancer contre le mur des trompettes?

Alors, comme un lévrier leurré, comme en lévrier fou qui commence à courir en lui-même, à courir, à courir en lui-même infatigablement, Agrigibi, désemparé, animé de vaines trépidations, <<s'élance en arrière>>, se perdant avec vertige dans les corridors interminables de son être.

Ici les heures de la Mna commandent.

A l'heure N, les ordres sont centaures, moitié pensées, moitié sur pattes. Comment faire? Entre révolte et rêve sont ses élans.

La complication a surgi dès le réveil. Cependant que

"The mirror of the soul," said Agrigibi, "sometimes sends me back as a dog, sometimes a crab, sometimes an ant, sometimes a spider, sometimes a weasel caught in a trap, sometimes a young hedgehog with soft prickles, sometimes a wounded mosquito with its wings torn off, in short my willingness is mocked, defeated like a creased note in a prostitute's stocking."

The jagged being, who then will speak in its name?

How many times does Agrigibi not meet tornadic beings! Strange? Hardly. It's with a continual thunder of triumph that the healthy advance everywhere, brother of the lion and the steamroller. With force he throws, through his skin, through his eyes, a carrousel of forks, to force, to pierce, to break weak points established tenuously themselves, which cannot bend the mechanism of the gust of wind that feels human and that is only spin, that whirlwind, that crushing, that persecution, that explosion, that ceaseless threat of explosion.

How to resist?

How to advance against the wall of trumpets?

So then, like a decoy greyhound, like a mad greyhound that begins to run inside itself, to run, to run in itself tirelessly, Agrigibi, helpless, animated by futile vibrations, "rushes backwards," getting lost with dizziness in the unending hallways of his being.

Here the hours of the Mna rule.

At the Nth hour, the orders are centaurs, half thoughts, half on foot. How? Its impulses are between revolt and dream.

The complication arose with reveille. While the bugles

retentissent les clairons, quel est mon camp? Quel est mon territoire? Derrière moi (ou à côte) je me mets à ma poursuite, objet de fièvre et de délire.

Avec quelle ardeur j'attends l'éclatement des fenêtres.

Désirs et turgescence écoutent grimper les octaves. Cependant la grade migration des barques a commencé. Une plus grande se prépare. Une très, très grande en vérité.

Celui qui aime sera fluvial. Est-ce cela, vraiment, qu'il a voulu? Est-ce bien cela, qui à demain le conduit, demain édifice par terre, demain hébété, demain comme une tomate écrasée?

Les phases de la vue ici sont telles: il y a d'abord quatre zones de gris où des colonnes de gris plus sombre se forment et s'entrecroisent: c'est le matin de l'œil, qui peut ne pas coïncider le moins du monde avec le matin du jour solaire et peut même arriver la nuit.

Selon les cas, il y a vue satisfaisante, devenant petit à petit savoureuse, ou simplement un petit chatouillement et même il peut manquer.

Vient ensuite par passages souples une clarté grandissante jusqu'au midi de l'œil, après quoi obscurcissement progressif jusqu'au soir de l'oeil.

La nuit de l'œil, elle n'arrive pas tous les jours. Certains sont réglés pour l'avoir à peine une fois l'an. D'autres, rares il est vrai, ne l'ont jamais connue pleinement. Mais si jamais elle leur vient, ce sera une installation pour des mois, et, eux, bien obligés, vivront cachés alors et retirés, comme des infirmes et comme des dégradés.

Ainsi est l'œil que ne suit pas la vie, ainsi est la vie que ne suit pas l'œil.

sound, which is my camp? What is my territory? Behind me (or to the side) I begin my pursuit, object of excitement and delirium.

With such ardor I wait for the windows to burst open.

Desires and turgescence listen to the octaves climbing. The large migration of small boats has begun however. An even larger one is being prepared. A very, very large one in fact.

☆

He who loves will be of the river. Is this, really, what he wanted? Is that right, tomorrow that drives him, tomorrow a building on the ground, tomorrow dazed, tomorrow like a crushed tomato?

☆

The phases of the view are these: first, there are four gray zones where columns of a darker gray are formed and intertwined: it's the morning of the eye, which may not coincide at all with the morning of the solar day, and can even happen at night.

Depending on the situation, there is a pleasing view, becoming more delightful little by little, or simply a small tickle can occur and will not be noticed.

Following next through flexible passages is a light that grows until the noon of the eye, after which there is a progressive darkening until the night of the eye.

The night of the eye doesn't come everyday. Some are set to have it just once a year at best. Others, although rare, have never known it at all. But if it ever comes to them, there will be an exhibition which lasts for months, and, they, clearly obliged, will come, previously hidden and drawn away, like the crippled and degraded.

Such is the eye that doesn't follow life, such is the life that doesn't follow the eye.

CORRESPONDANCE

CARTE 1

L'eau du Golfe est chaude, toujours chaude. Ça poissonne partout. Bribdolette fait bien, mais faut pas être piètre avec elle. N'est pas pour chercher des obstacles, tu comprends, mais la trigue ça l'embête, c'est tout.

Mahouque bien.

L'Omerose, tu auras des ennuis avec.

CARTE II

Ici tout parle de haut, vient de loin, s'arrête court. Pas moyen pourtant de se passer du chapeau. On se fait conduire du grand au plus grand. Du plus grand au plus grand encore. Ensuite on pourra ramasser tous les petits.

En ce moment on est avec les Davas. Épaule à épaule. De là on passe chez les Tarasses. Les Tarasses de Bloubios. Toujours égaux, toujours frères. On échange ses roues. Ensuite les Prissis de Oppropisis. Il le faut. Et le clan des Abbrassias sera acquis. Toujours égaux, toujours à niveau. Après, c'est différent. Après, les têtes pourront changer.

En attendant, faut y mettre du nôtre, de l'huile, tu saisis ? Ne réponds pas à l'épinette. Réponds franchement. Je ne suis pas venu ici pour traire les papayers.

CORRESPONDENCE

CARD 1

The water from the Gulf is hot, always hot. It swells with fish. Bribdolette is doing well, but you must not be feeble with her. It's not about looking for obstacles, you understand, but it's the intrigue that bothers her, that's all.

Mahouque is good.

You will have trouble with the Omerose.

CARD II

Here, everything speaks of above, comes from afar, stops short. No means however of passing the buck along. You guide yourself from great to greater. From greater to even greater yet. Then, you will be able to gather all who are small.

At the moment, we are with the Davas. Shoulder to shoulder. From there we are going to see the Tarasses. The Tarasses from Bloubios. Always equal, always brothers. We exchange wheels. Next are the Prissis from Oppropisis. That's a necessity. And the tribe from Abbrassias will be taken. Always equal, always up to standard. Afterwards, it's different. After, heads will be able to change.

In the meantime, we have to put some of our oil on it, you understand? Don't reply with a tune. Reply frankly. I haven't come here to milk the papayas.

CARTE III

Je parle en homme, pas en oiseau de cage. Laisse le marais puant. Je n'ai pas de jalousie. Je ne le connais pas, ton Ottolutre. Qui s'occupe d'un insecte, s'il n'en est gratté ? Le nœud de la situation est ici. Je ranimerai la branche morte. Sinon au feu et pas de criaillement. Je ne veux pas d'une soudure molle. Ça lâche toujours au mauvais moment et on se retrouve tous par terre illico.

CARTE IV

Qu'as-tu encore ? On dirait que tu es tout trempé. Fais les taire, bon sang. On ne demande pas leur avis. Je ne veux pas de la cérémonie des bouches ouvertes, moi. Tu les stoppes, tu entends, et tout de suite. Ne perds pas ta proue dans les roseaux.

CARD III

I speak as a man, not a bird in a cage. Leave the stink-ing marsh. I'm not jealous. I don't know him, your Ot-tolutre. Who takes care of an insect, if he isn't scratched by it? The crux of the situation is here. I will bring the dead branch back to life. Otherwise in the fire, and no weeping. I don't want a soft welding. It always falls apart at the worst moment and you find yourself on the ground, pronto.

CARD IV

What's wrong with you now? Looks like you are drenched. Make them be quiet, damn it. We didn't ask for their opinion. I don't want a fuss from wide open mouths. You stop them, you hear, and now. Don't lose your bow in the reeds.

CARTE V

Lippa écarté.

Dot écartée.

Glemméche écarté.

Oui, oui, les prouesses, je ne dis pas, mais des échelons, ce n'est pas encore l'échelle. Ausculte le brave, tu trouves un sourd. Et qu'est-ce, dis donc, que j'peux faire d'un sourd ?

Risia écartée et comment ! Je ne t'écoute pas. Perds pas ta salive. Te retourne pas sur cette trille en l'air. Je ne reviens jamais à l'allée abandonnée.

Orquendon, pourquoi je ne l'ai pas garde ? Il manque d'étau si tu veux savoir. Ses exploits, c'est toujours tomber dessus, rouler dedans, c'est ça, ses aventures. Où as-tu vu qu'il tenait les manettes ? Il manque d'étau j'te dis. Quel emploi j'aurais, dis, pour un bouchon que l'eau remue ?

CARTE VI

Ta lettre me soufflette au visage. Tu vas me dire que tu t'es trompé. Tu n'es qu'un veau flageolant. Je vomis sur ta figure, voilà ce que j'en fais de ta figure. Et ne reparle plus de Vena. Les points les plus éloignés sont proches, quand un être est blessé et s'ouvre à la vengeance. Tais-toi, brouillon, et ne cherche pas à tout faire à la fois et à donner avis ici, où tu ne connais rien.

Je retournerai, à cheval, au pays, tu peux en être sûr. Bientôt, je tiendrai tous les rameaux dans ma main. Alors, il sera temps, pas maintenant.

Écoute les vivants d'abord et puis tu répondras aux morts. Souviens-t'en, agite du dernier verre. Je ne suis pas un concombre, moi, et le sang, tu devrais le savoir, coule aisément de la poitrine des faibles. Il coule abondant et

CARD V

Lippa dismissed.

Dot discarded.

Glemmeche dismissed.

Yes, yes, quite the feat, I don't deny that, but the standards are not yet up to scale. Examine the brave, and you will find one who is deaf. Then you might say, what can I do with someone who's deaf?

Risia discarded and how! I'm not listening to you. Don't waste your breath. Don't come back on this trill in the air. I never come back to an abandoned alley.

Orquendon, why didn't I keep him? He lacked a good grip if you must know. His exploits, always falling in, rolling around inside, that's it, his adventures. Did you see where he held the levers? I'm telling you, he lacks a solid grip. What use would I have then, for a plug the water can remove?

CARD VI

Your letter slapped me in the face. You're going to tell me that you were mistaken. You're just a trembling calf. I vomit on your face, there that's what I'm doing to your face. And don't talk about Vena anymore. The furthest points are close when a being is injured and opens himself up to revenge. Shut up, meddler, and stop looking to do everything all at once and giving your opinion when you don't know anything.

I'll come back, on horseback, to the country, you can be sure of it. Soon, I'll hold all of the palm leaves in my hand. It will be time then, not now.

Listen to the living first, and then you will respond to the dead. Remember this, shaken from the night-cap. I am not a cucumber, and the blood, you should know, flows easily from the chests of the weak. It flows abundantly, and

eux, les voilà sur le sol étendus à tout jamais. J'en ai connu d'autres, des bavards, qui se sont tus, la langue pendante sur le carreau, qui n'avaient pas su la tenir fermée leur petite gueule, qu'ils croyaient si solide.

they lay sprawled out on the ground until the end of time. I have known others, gossips who fell silent, their tongues, which they had thought to be so solid, but which could never stay in their little mouths, lay hanging out onto the floor.

DANS L'ESPACE
LA VIE PARCELLAIRE

LES QUATRE OBSERVATEURS

Donc solidement fixé
il observe
lui, le block, le un
le parfaitement bien braqué
le Charlemagne des machines
abaissant son œil, appareil de conquête . . .
Le deux aussi est la
changeur
arrangeur
commerçant d'images
prêt à être femme s'il le faut
à être l'autre s'il le faut
à être paillasse s'il le faut
Judas qui va se trahir pour l'image
Opération troc et monnaie
Le trois aussi est la
le dédouble, le deux en une personne
la triple sphère
le quarré sur trois points et sur sept piliers
l'équilibré, le souple, le phoque
l'être des arrivages réguliers
des plans inclinés
des écarts combinés
celui qui prélève
qui repartit
qui échelonne
. . . et le spectacle soumis, par paliers, vient à lui

IN SPACE
THE FRAGMENTED LIFE

THE FOUR OBSERVERS

Then solidly fixed
he watches
him, the block, the one
perfectly aimed
the Charlemagne of machines
lowering his eye, conquering device . . .
The second is also here
money changer
arranger
image dealer
ready to be a woman if necessary
to be the other if necessary
to be a clown if necessary
Judas who will betray himself for the image
Operation swap and currency
The third is also here
the double, the two in one person
triple sphere
the argument on three points and seven pillars
the equilibrium, the supple, the seal
the being of regular deliveries
of inclined planes
combined differences
he who takes
who distributes
who spaces things out at intervals
. . . and the spectacle, presented in stages, comes to him

Opération calcul
Le quatre, le quatre aussi est la
ennoué, embarrassé, emmatelassé
tantôt dans des cordes, tantôt dans brumes
cherchant problème dans « pas de problème »
et rêverie et caresses dans problème
Opération vents
. . . *mais qui va baratter ?*
Dessous, tranquille au milieu d'eux
divisé comme un empire
commun comme des compères
dense comme une meule
dispersé comme des flocons

Calculated operation
The fourth, the fourth is also here
tied up, embarrassed, padded
sometimes in strings, sometimes in fog
looking for the problem in "there's no problem"
and dreams and caresses the problem
Operation of winds
. . . but who will churn?
Below, quiet in their midst
divided as an empire
common as accomplices
dense as a millstone
dispersed like snowflakes

retranché comme un fort
ouvert comme des arènes
l'objet gît entre les observateurs
Toutefois chaque témoin
lui-même est quatre
quatre écartelés
cherchant à devenir « un »
par la grâce de l'objet en spectacle
qui semble simple
qui semble un
qui semble autonome
qui semble fixe
mais, qui, observé

entrenched like one who is strong
open like the arenas
the object lies between the observers
However each witness
himself is four
four torn
looking to be "one"
by the grace of the object in sight
which seems simple
which seems as one
seems autonomous
which seems fixed
but, which, observed

se met à montrer des parties
et à partir en morceaux
à osciller de-ci de-là, à brinquebaler
à se conjoindre en jumelages, en appariements scandaleux
(ou remarquables ou beaux ou cocasses)
dans des lieux lointains
ou à se perdre sur place, objet pailleté, dans la lumière
objet excessif
objet en démangeaison d'objets
en litanie d'objets
en laitance d'objets
en panorama d'objets
en mer d'objets
d'objets
d'objets
d'objets
ainsi que ledit observateur lui-même
objet
objets
objets
objets . . .

starts to show its parts
and then in pieces
turns from here to there, jolted along
to be united in twinning, in outrageous pairings
(or remarkable or beautiful or comical)
in distant places
or loses itself on the spot, spangled object, in the light
excessive object
object in itching of objects
in a litany of objects
in a milt of objects
in a panorama of objects
in a sea of objects
of objects
of objects
of objects
as well as the said observer himself
object
objects
objects . . .

THE THIN MAN

Petit
petit sous le vent
petit et lacunaire
pressé et sachant que vite il faut qu'il sache
petit, particulier, dans sa petite galaxie
veillant
faisant perpétuellement le quart
dans son automoteur, son autocorrecteur
dans son peu de paix
dans son pas de paix du tout
bruissant sous la douche de milliers d'avertisseurs
sonné
sassé
sifflé
frappé
percé
se croyant de la chair
se voulant dans un palais
mais vivant dans des palans
innombrable et frêle
horloger cependant
et fœtus aussi commandant dans les rafales
visé
entamé
abordé
agrippé
agriffé
frappé à coups redoublés
gravé comme une plaque
cliquetant comme un télescripteur
déplacé
dévié

THE THIN MAN

Small
small in the wind
small and lacunary
hurried and knowing that quickly he must know
small, particular, in his own galaxy
watching
and by doing so, perpetually in fourths
in his automotor, his autocorrecter
in his little amount of peace
in his no peace at all
rustling under the shower of a thousand alarms
sounded
sifted
whistled
struck
pierced
thinking himself flesh
wishing himself in a palace
but living in the pulleys
countless and fragile
a watchmaker nonetheless
and a fetus as well, commanding through the squalls
aimed at
broken into
boarded
grabbed
clawed
struck with redoubled blows
engraved like a plaque
clicking like a teletype
displaced
diverted

son miroir mille fois brisé
affolé
à l'écoute
ne voulant pas être perdu
traçant des plans
des plans se traçant en lui
des plans contradictoires
des plan étrangers
des plans rebondissant
des plans à l'infini
luttant avec des plans
jamais tout à fait submergé
et même il va bientôt sourire
et puis croire que la vie est bonheur et soupirs
et doux corps rapprochés,
dans des cordes tendues
et des notes éperdues
puis à nouveau renversé
redressé
puis de nouveau alerté
en danger d'être arrêté
assèché
épuisé
refaisant des plans,
des contre-plans
des plans d'oppositions
dans l'obscur
dans le futur
dans l'indéterminé
pilote
pilote tant qu'il pourra
pilote jusqu'à la fin
pilote ou plus rien
cible en plein vol qui scrute
qui traçe des plans,

his mirror broken a thousand times
frightened
listening
not wanting to be lost
drawing plans
of the plans drawing themselves in him
contradictory plans
foreign plans
plans bouncing back
infinite plans
struggling with plans
never quite submerged
and he will even smile soon
and then believe that life is happiness and sighs
and soft bodies brought close together,
in taught strings
and distraught notes
then again reversed
straightened
then a new alarm
in danger of being stopped
drained
exhausted
redoing plans,
counter-plans
plans of oppositions
in obscurity
into futurity
in indeterminacy
a pilot
pilot as long as he can
pilot until the end
pilot or nothing else
a target in midflight who scrutinizes
who draws plans,

encore des plans
des plans . . .

Celui qui est né dans la nuit
souvent refera son Mandala

more plans
plans . . .

He who was born in the night
again and again will remake his Mandala

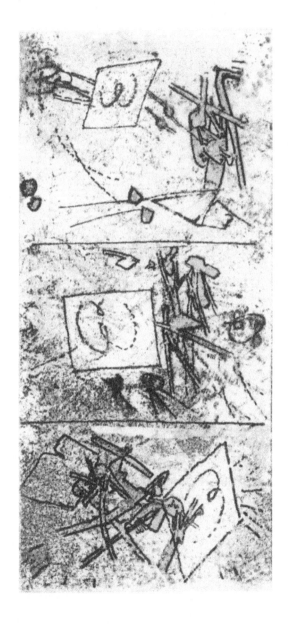

BOUCLIER SOUS LES COUPS

Sous l'averse qui pleut sur lui
sous la projection incessante
dans le bouillonnement
il reçoit
il reçoit quoi ?
Difficile savoir
difficile savoir savoir
Derrière quatre écrans
dans sa chambre noire
il reçoit
Les prises sont multiples
les abandons sont multiples
Entre douze savoirs, onze fois le doute
et le vent,
le vent de l'infime
le vent venant de l'inconnu
le vent de l'incertitude
le vent pour la perpétuation de l'incertitude.
Ubiquité par les voix
par les sons
par les lendemains qui avancent et crient déjà
Ubiquité par les restes de vieux enfantements
par les braillements contemporains
par les absences récalcitrantes
qui réclament présence, intime judicieuse présence.
Trouble maintenant
trouble semblable à une paix bousculée
paix semblable à des éléphants de mer
sur une plage inhospitalière
Pouvoirs réduits.
plus de pouvoirs
poussière de pouvoirs
pluie de pluie

SHIELD UNDER BLOWS

Under the downpour which rains on him
under the incessant splashing
in the bubbling
he receives
what does he receive?
Difficult knowledge
difficult knowledge to know
Behind four screens
in his darkroom
he receives
The takes are multiple
the abandonments are multiple
Between 12 times knowing, 11 times doubting
and the wind,
the infinitesimal wind
wind coming from the unknown
the wind of uncertainty
the wind for the perpetuation of uncertainty.
Ubiquity through voices
through sounds
through tomorrows that advance and shout already
Ubiquity through the remains of old births
through contemporary howls
through recalcitrant absences
that require presence, intimate shrewd presence.
Trouble now
trouble similar to a peace turned upside down
peace similar to sea elephants
on an inhospitable beach
Reduced powers.
more powers
dust of powers
rain of rain

vertiges
buisson de pales
qui file
qui a filé
efforts finis . . .
L'observatoire précieux a plongé dans la mer des sens.

Temps
temps s'écoule
manne de temps
quel temps ?

vertigo
bush of blades
that flees
that had fled
finished efforts . . .
The precious observatory plunged into the sea of senses.

Time
time passes
manna of time
what time?

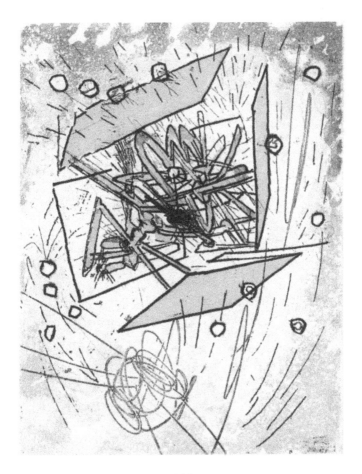

Cependant du tréfonds un appareil volant sans cesse s'élève
sur les cercles de l'être endormi
C'est l'heure où le pauvre et le déchu
comme le riche et l'important
recueille une moisson-surprise dans des champs inconnus
où chacun, de retour chez soi, vit avec ses parasites
mais balai à son tour balayé
reviennent les dehors
se rapprochent les dehors on perçoit
on perçoit
on perçoit qu'on perçoit
afflux
Afflux sur soi
afflux contre afflux
Et prédateur comprend

Soleil a qui sait réunir

From the depths however an incessantly flying apparatus arises
over the circles of the sleeping being
It is the hour where the poor and the fallen
like the rich and the important
gather a surprise harvest in unknown fields
where each, upon returning home, lives with its parasites
but a broom swept in turn
brings the outside in
the outside coming closer
one perceives
one perceives that one perceives
surge
Surge of oneself
surge against surge
And predator understands

Sun that is able to reunite

QUATRE
CENTS
HOMMES
EN CROIX

mil neuf cent cinquante six

FOUR HUNDRED MEN ON THE CROSS

nineteen fifty-six

HENRI

MICHAUX

FOUR   HUNDRED

M
E
N

ON

THE

C
R
O
S
S

NINETEEN

FIFTY-SIX

Journal d'un dessinateur

FRAGMENTS

(DESSINS ENTREPRIS EN 1953)

JE
NE PEUX PAS TOUJOURS PLACER LA CROIX D'ABORD.

PARFOIS C'EST L'HOMME qu'il faut étendre avant tout, étendre en plein ciel, mais étendre, étendre, comme s'étend la peine des hommes.

122

Diary of a Draftsman

FRAGMENTS
(DRAWINGS MADE IN 1953)

I CANNOT ALWAYS PLACE THE CROSS FIRST.

SOMETIMES IT'S THE MAN who must be stretched out before everything else, stretched out in the middle of the sky, stretched and stretched, the way human suffering stretches.

Celui-ci, un être oublié sur une croix. On l'y a perdu.

Celui-là, un homme volant, qu'on aurait stoppé, brutalement STOPPÉ.

Cet autre, une sorte de long moucheron, épinglé sur une croix interminablement haute, d'où parler aux hommes serait de toutes façons, absolument impossible, absolument vain.

Celui-ci encore un insecte. Ne compte pas. Même en croix un insecte pourrait-il sauver le genre humain?

This one's forgotten on a cross. Someone lost him there.

That one's a flying man, who seems to have been stopped, abruptly STOPPED.

And that one is a sort of long gnat pinned to a cross that goes up interminably high, from where it would, in any case, be completely impossible, completely pointless to talk to men.

This one's another insect. Doesn't count. Even on the cross, could an insect save the human race?

Le 42, un voyou.

Le 51, canard, véritable coin-coin en croix.

[53] Christ peut-être, le premier qui apparaisse sur la croix, mais furieux d'y être. Sur le bois courtaud, il essaye avec de grands efforts de dégager ses bras, ses mains (comme sanglées) prêtes à filer par-dessus la traverse, larges et nerveuses. Christ ou parachutiste?

(54) Celui-ci, qu'on n'essaye pas de tirer de lui de l'espérance.
Son expression:
LA MORT POUR RIEN,
pour augmenter l'erreur.

Number 42, a lout.

Number 51, duck, a real quack-quacking on the cross.

[53] Christ perhaps, the first to appear on the cross, but furious at being there. On squat wood, he makes huge efforts to free his arms, his hands (as though strapped) are broad and nervous and look ready to run on top of the crossbar. Christ or parachutist?

(54) Don't try to get any hope from this one.
His expression:
DEATH FOR NOTHING,
just increases the error.

(60) Intense, intense, d'un intense tel qu'il en est devenu flammes. Sûrement il va consumer la croix. Fut-ce par le feu, décidé à

<<en sortir>>

Pas douteux: Ni les uns ni les autres ne veulent de la passion. Ils ne marchent pas. Ne croient pas au rachat par la croix. Ne l'envisagent pas.

|72| Après plus de soixante-dix crucifixions, <<il>> n'accepte pas encore d'étendre les bras, d'étendre les deux, encore moins de les laisser attachés. Il <<lui>> faut au moins, encore que ça ne serve à rien, en dégager un.

Même si la main reste solidement clouée d'un clou gros comme un rivet, il s'arrange pour faire de son bras un arc outrancier qui va défaire la suspension, l'ordonnance générale et presque le crucifiement lui-même qu'on pouvait cette fois juger accepté et définitif.

(60)   Intense, intense, so intense that he burst into flames. He's sure to consume the cross. By fire if necessary, he decides to

"get out of this"

No doubt: Neither man nor the cross want the passion. They don't co-operate. They don't believe in redemption through the cross. Don't see it.

|72| After more than seventy crucifixions, "he" still cannot bring himself to spread out the arms, spread them both out, still less leave them bound. "He" must at least leave one arm free, pointless as that is.

Even though the hand remains firmly nailed down with a great nail like a rivet, he makes sure the arm forms an extravagant curve to distort the suspension, the overall layout, and almost the crucifixion itself, which can now be deemed accepted and final.

SOIXANTE-SEIZE

Si extrême est son effort d'évasion, qu'il semble, tant va loin l'étirement de ses membres, (sa tête cependant presqu'entièrement rentrée dans ses épaules) que c'est au bout du monde qu'il est allé chercher des bras pour y pendre son corps misérable, qui le fait tant souffrir, bras interminables qui ont véritablement fui en longueur et par une infinie extension ont tenté le refuge dans l'espace.

QUATRE-VINGT-TROIS

Secret,
ployé,
plongé,
tordu

                                    déserteur.

(84) Un cherche-querelle

SEVENTY-SIX

So extreme is his effort to escape, his limbs stretched to such a point (although his head is almost entirely sunk in his shoulders), that it looks as though he went to the ends of the earth to find arms from which to hang his miserable body that causes him such suffering—interminable arms that have positively fled out sideways and have tried to seek refuge through endless extension in space.

EIGHTY-THREE

Secret,
bowed,
sunk,
twisted

deserter.

(84) A quarrel-seeker

Un enragé à vouloir, non reposer sur la croix, mais marcher dessus, telle qu'elle est, à moitié dressée.

Pendant que les vociférateurs au pied de la croix l'insultent,

lui, furieux, hors de lui, mais non pour autant hors de <<ça>>, cherche, pieds libérés, un commencement de plancher dans le montant de la croix, pour se détendre afin de pouvoir ensuite s'en aller et tourner les talons à toute cette affaire qui ne l'intéresse pas, dont décidément il ne veut plus.

QUATRE-VINGT-SEPT

Avec quel infini repliement il se tapit en lui-même, au fond de ce corps dont malignement on a attrapé certaines parties, certaines connexions, pour les fixer sur un bois impossible, un bois de solive qui ne reconnaît pas les prophètes et qui en tenant un ne le lâchera plus.

88

Refuge dans la lassitude. La CROIX elle-même flotte avec L U I   d a n s   u n   b r o u i l l a r d   i n f i n i .

EIGHTY-FIVE

A madman to want, not to rest on the cross but to walk over it, as it is, half-raised.

While the people clamoring at the base of the cross insult him,

                                    he is furious, beside himself, but not so beside "that," his feet freed, he seeks the beginning of a floor on the upright post of the cross so that he can relax, and then go away, and turn his back on this business which doesn't interest him and which he definitely wants nothing more to do with.

EIGHTY-SEVEN

With what infinite withdrawal he retreats into himself, to the depths of this body, some parts, some links of which have been cruelly seized, tied to impossible wood, the wood of joists that do not recognize the prophets and which, now that they hold one, will not let him go.

88

Refuge in the lassitude. The CROSS itself floats with H I M   i n   u n e n d i n g   f o g .

QUATRE-VINGT-ONZE.
Ses bras en parasol retombent
en pluie sur la plaine des
hommes. Un peu çivaïte.

93

Fantôme
en l'air,
fantôme
malheureux
qui fait apparaître une croix,
fantomale comme lui
d'abord une tache,
une vaste tache
s'agrandissant
en croix
démesurée,
croix pour
l'humanité
entière.

NINETY-ONE
His arms like an umbrella fall
down as rain on the plain of
men. A little Shiva.

93

Ghost
in the air,
wretched
ghost
who conjures up a cross,
ghostly like him,
at first a mark,
a huge mark
that grows
into a giant
cross,
cross for
the whole of
humanity.

|97| Étrange dévouement. La croix menaçait de tomber en morceaux, certainement allait lâcher, sans <<ses>> bras, qui par une folle idée de sacrifice (ou par un réflexe mal placé) ont maintenu le bois pourri, ont sauvé la croix et la cérémonie et l'holocauste, répondant ainsi matériellement à ce qu'on attendait de lui.

Non sur,   [99]
mais dans *la*
croix, à l'interieur
des barreaux de laquelle,

Lui dedans,   *il se laise observer*
tout au fond,
petit,   *comme dans une cellule*
rétréci,   *de prison, indifférent*
nié, raturé,   *d'une facon, déchiré*
presque
insaisissable.   *de l'autre. Grosse*

est la croix, bedonnante,
comme si de plusieurs
futures croix elle
allait accou-
cher.

138

|97| Curious
devotion.   The
cross was in danger of falling a-
part, seemed certain to let go,
without "his" arms, which in a crazy
idea of sacrifice
(or by a re-
flex misplaced)
held firm the
rotten wood, and
saved the cross
and the ceremony
and the holocaust,
thereby answering
m a t e r i a l l y
what was ex-
pected of him.

Not on,   [99]
but in *the*
cross, inside
whose bars he allows

He is inside,   *himself to be observed*
at the very bottom, *as though in a prison*
small,
shrunken,   *cell, indifferent*
disclaimed, erased, *in one way, torn apart*
almost
imperceptible. *in another. Fat*

the cross is, paunchy,
as if to so many
future crosses it
was giving
birth.

139

HOMME-CROIX. Tout à la fois le soutien et le soutenu, le souffrant et l'instrument de la souffrance.

La croix enfin s'est mise à souffrir. Le drame entre en elle. La voilà qui s'affole. Elle a compris. Elle ne peut plus se retenir. Elle aussi va proclamer.

Le monde entier devra se tordre dans la souffrance du sacrifice.

QUI désormais pourra se réfugier loin de la douleur?

212

```
                    Christ
                   en filin.
                   Plus que
                    de la
                    corde.
Tout ce qui reste de lui, une corde fixée sur une croix.
                   Pas de
                  spectacle.
                     Ce
                     qui
                   compte
                     est
                  ailleurs.
```

104

MAN-CROSS. At once the support and the supported, the sufferer and the instrument of suffering.

The cross has at last begun to suffer. Tragedy descends on it. Now it is distraught. It has understood. It can no longer hold back. It, too, is going to proclaim.

The whole world must writhe in the suffering of the sacrifice.

WHO, from now on, can hide far from grief?

212

Christb
as a cable.
More than
the rope.
All that remains of him, a rope fixed to a cross.
No
spectacle.
What
matters
is
elsewhere.

EN CELUI-CI, C'EST LA TÊTE QUI EST LE GROS BLOC, LE BLOC NON ÉQUARRI, DUR, RUDE, ÉNORME, QUI DOIT RESTER ENTIER, PRÉSERVÉ. QUI EST CONTRE *la sinuosité des hommes, leurs danses, leurs allées et venues, leur évolution.* TÊTE SOMBRE, MASSIVE, RABOTEUSE, BLOC QUI DIT TOUJOURS CE QU'IL DIT UNE FOIS.

(230) Ratatiné, gueux, gueule noire, gibbon rasé, incroyablement concentré. Après ce recueillement insensé, surhumain, le hérissement de tout le haut de l'être en pointes pugnaces, en flèches d'illumination, est-ce une couronne?

215 IN THIS ONE, IT'S THE HEAD THAT IS THE MAIN BLOCK, A BLOCK ROUGH HEWN, HARD, RUGGED, HUGE, WHICH MUST REMAIN WHOLE, PRESERVED. WHICH COUNTERS *the sinuosity of people, their dances, their comings and goings, their evolution.* DARK HEAD, MASS-IVE, UNEVEN, BLOCK THAT STILL SAYS WHAT IT ONCE SAID.

(230) Shriveled, wretched, black maw, shaven gibbon, incredibly concentrated. After this insane, superhuman contemplation, the whole upper part of the man bristles in belligerent spikes, arrows of illumination: is it a crown?

[232]

```
F       p       s       p       d       c       e       l
r       a       e       r       i       h       n       a
a       r       s       o       s       a               n
p                       p       c       ng              i
p                       r       i       é               è
é                       e       p       s               r
                        s       l                       e
                                e                       s
                        s
```

m a i s   t r è s   r e c o n n a i s s a b l e s . . .

(254) S'il priait Dieu, ce serait pour qu'on éloigne la foule.

DEUX-CENT-CINQUANTE-SEPT

Un penseur, un retiré du monde, un être qui médite et ne s'aperçoit pas qu'il est en croix, (ou) qui a repoussé la tentation de croire qu'on l'a mis en croix, (ou) qui ne veut plus être distrait par des histoires de croix, un homme qui monte ses degrés.

144

[232]

```
S    b    h    o    d    t    i    l
t    y    i    w    i    u    n    a
r         s    n    s    r    t    s
u                   c    n    o    h
c                   i    e         e
k                   p    d         s
                    l
               e
          s
```

but thoroughly recognizable . . .

(254) If he prayed to God, it would be for the crowd to be sent away.

TWO-HUNDRED-AND-FIFTY-SEVEN

A thinker, a recluse, a contemplative who does not notice that he is on the cross (or) who has rejected the temptation to believe that he has been put on the cross (or) who no longer wants to be distracted by anything to do with the cross, a man who ascends his steps.

Un petit ange noir, pas plus grand qu'un orvet, minuscule corps à sept fouets fins (pas besoin d'ailes tant il est follement véloce) donc l'infernalement alerte, en suspens dans l'air, le petit ange, dispos, dégagé, suractif, derrière la croix, est apparu.

260

A l'oreille de la forme effondrée, il dit le Secret de Vie. Dans un tremblement agile, le message est transmis. C'est fait. Au crucifié maintenant de décider, au destin . . .

A little black angel, no bigger
than a slowworm, a tiny body with seven
260   delicate whips (no need for wings, he's so
crazily swift), and so devilishly
alert, hanging in the air, the little
angel, fit, casual, hyperactive, has appeared behind the cross.

Into the ear of the crumpled figure, he mutters the Secret of Life. With a deft tremor, the message is transmitted. It is done. Now, it is for the crucified man to decide, for fate . . .

LONG ARRÊT.

Des mois.

Je viens de recommencer et . . . recommence aussitôt leur répugnance à se mettre en croix.

C'est raté.

Absence d'abandon, efforts toujours pour s'arracher, ou pour s'accroupir sur la croix, pour se distraire durant ces heures pénibles. Aucun respect pour la mise en scène du Golgotha.

Visiblement ils sont là en étrangers, en résistants. Ils ne voient pas ainsi le salut, ne pensent pas le gagner pour les autres, ne se connaissent pas de père dans le ciel, ni de fils sur la terre.

Soit! Faisons alors simplement des croix. Croix, signe simple, mais vaste, où tout entre et est tenu en respect, évocateur suffisamment et pudique au moins.

Excellent. C'est la solution.

Tout de même après quelque temps une croix à nouveau <<attire>> un corps . . . qui ne convient pas. Un deuxième . . . qui ne convient pas, un troisième, un quatrième. Impossible de les arrêter, entraîné par l'habitude acquise, perdant mon temps à mettre en croix des gens qui n'y croient pas, qui y restent distraits, n'ont rien à y faire, ne songent qu'à en descendre, m'occupant stupidement à appliquer à la forme pure de la croix les formes impures de l'homme, sa masse encore plus impure, son contenu encore plus impur, qui menace de bientôt venir au-dehors, sale et dégoulinant.

Months.

I've just begun again and . . . instantly, their reluctance to be put on the cross begins again.

It's a failure.

Lack of renunciation, still these efforts to get away, or to crouch over the cross, to find distractions during these difficult hours. No respect for the setting of Golgotha.

They're clearly here as outsiders, as resistors. Consequently, they cannot see salvation, don't think they're gaining it for others, don't know about a father in heaven or a son on earth.

All right! Let's just make crosses, then. The cross, a simple sign, but huge, where everything enters and is kept a respectful distance, evocative enough and modest at least.

Excellent. That's the answer.

All the same, after a while, a cross "calls for" a body again. . . but it's not right. A second. . . which is not right, a third, a fourth. Impossible to stop them, driven by ingrained habit, wasting my time putting people on the cross who don't believe in it, who look absent, have nothing to do with it, whose one thought is to get down from it, dumbly spending my time applying to the pure form of the cross the impure forms of man, his bulk more impure still, his contents even more impure and in danger of spilling out, foul and dripping.

Il faudrait

UN HOMME
CRISTAL

What's needed

A CRYSTAL
MAN

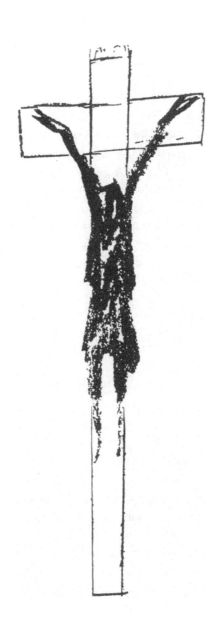

UNI À LUI, entouré des images de Lui en croix, trouvant toute vie profonde en Lui, par Lui, avec Lui, préférablement à tout autre être au monde, mais cela il y a longtemps, c'était dans les années graves de ma vie, dans mon adolescence . . .

A présent, quelle différence! Mais l'idée m'était venue, [idée basse] de retenir par le dessin. Celui à qui j'avais été lié autrefois par l'ardeur et la foi. Tel était le projet.

Minable resurrection! A quel point je m'étais éloigné de Lui, éloigné à ne plus pouvoir me le représenter* (son sens, sa mission, l'oblation consentie) je le savais à présent et n'aurais pu mieux le savoir d'une autre façon.

* Je devrais essayer le Bouddha peut-être, plus récent en moi, et sinon vivant, moins exclu que l'homme du Calvaire.

. . . SI J'ÉTAIS DIRECTEUR DE SÉMINAIRE, la piété, l'obéissance, les exercices spirituals bien, bien,

mais c'est au dessin que je les attendrais mes zélés séminaristes. Les dessins du crucifié que je les obligerais de faire, talent ou non, d'une façon ou d'une autre, maladroitement, pauvrement, (d'autant plus parlants, plus fatalement parlants) m'en apprendraient plus que les confessions d'une année entière, ces trop faciles confessions en mots. Ils ne pourraient plus tricher, se mentir à eux-mêmes sur leur vocation.

Plus de refuge.

La, je <<cueillerais>> leur indifférence, leur sécheresse, leurs blasphèmes.

UNITED WITH HIM, surrounded by images of Him on the cross, finding all meaningful life in Him, through Him, with Him, in preference to all other beings on earth, but that was long ago, that was in the serious years of my life, in my adolescence . . .

What a difference now! But the idea had occurred to me [base idea] to hold on to the Man to whom I was once bound by passion and faith,in drawing. That was the plan.

Shabby resurrection! How far had I wandered from Him, so far that I could no longer represent him* (his meaning, his mission, the oblation granted), now I knew and could not have known better in any other way.

* Maybe I should try Buddha, more recent in me, and if not alive, then less excluded than the man of Calvary.

. . . IF I WERE A SEMINARY DIRECTOR, piety, obedience, spiritual exercises, fine, fine

but it's drawing I'd expect of my zealous seminarists. The drawings of the crucified man I'd make them do, with or without talent, one way or another, clumsily, badly (all the more eloquent, more inevitably eloquent), which would teach me more than the confessions of a whole year, those facile confessions in words. They wouldn't be able to cheat any more, to lie to themselves about their vocation.

No more refuge.

In that way, I'd "collect" their indifference, their hard-heartedness, their blasphemies.

Implacablement
les trahirait la LOI DES RÉSISTANCES INTÉRIEURES,
des RÉSISTANCES SECRÈTES, et deviendrait claire
la raison de l''échec partiel de leurs études religieuses
où, apparemment appliqués, ils n'arrivent pas cependant
à <<comprendre>> certaines matières de la foi, id est:
n'arrivent pas à les <<prendre avec eux>>, ne le veulent
pas, les ont, sans le savoir, en horreur, objets de scandale et
de vomissement.

POURRAIENT quelquefois ces dessins servir de
purgation. Qui sait? Libérés des images qui leur bouchaient
depuis longtemps peut-être le chemin et la vue du visage
autrefois aimé, il leur serait donné ainsi d'y revenir, etc.,
etc., s'il en est temps encore.

> Douteux.
> Extrêmement douteux.
> L'inverse plus souvent.
> Rendant définitif.

FIN

Relentlessly
THE LAW OF INTERNAL RESISTANCE would betray
them, THE LAW OF SECRET RESISTANCE, and the
reason for the partial failure of their religious studies would
become clear, for, despite their apparent studiousness, they
cannot "understand" certain matters of faith, they cannot
"take to them," don't want to; without realizing it, they
have a horror of them, are scandalized and nauseated by
them.

MIGHT these drawings sometimes serve as a purging?
Who knows? Freed of images that had maybe long been
blocking their way and view of the erstwhile cherished
face, they would thus find themselves able to return to it,
etc., etc., if there is still time.

> Doubtful.
> Highly doubtful.
> The opposite, more often.
> Making it final.

END

NOTES ON TRANSLATION

This translation would have been impossible without the conversation, guidance, incisive suggestion and careful reading of Jim Brook, Norma Cole, François Luong, and Donald Revell. Thank you all.

I would also like to thank Lee Briccetti and Stephen Motika at Poet's House in New York, who invited me to give a talk on Michaux, an occasion that resulted in my discovery of these texts and the immediate wish to translate them. This book is indebted to Margaret Rigaud-Drayton's *Henri Michaux: Poetry, Painting, and the Universal Sign,* her ideas on Michaux's complex relations between the visual and the verbal, and his life-long desire for a universal language.

A special thank you to Garrett Caples, for your steady support, good will, and excitement in and for this project.

Michaux wrote in the most transparent language possible, distrusting language too much to give it free reign. In some ways, this makes him an easy poet to translate. He did have his idiosyncrasies, however, in that he often slipped from the idiomatic or vernacular into a more formal literary French. Like many poets, he liked to invent words ("çivaïte" for "Shiva"? perhaps "Shiva-esque"?). Tonally, he can shift quite suddenly from delicacy, humor, and fragility to an arch anger or skepticism. In *Four Hundred Men on the Cross*, forming the poems into English from their original French shapes (as the book first appeared with Pierre Bettencourt's hand press) provided the most difficulty, a challenge made much easier by computer technology finally having caught up with the spacing capable of the human hand.

Henri Michaux would probably be the first to call all translations impossible tasks, viewing, as he did, all lan-

guages to be flawed and lacking. In translating him, I often found this skepticism to be a kind of belief, a hopeless hope in which, if all errors were mine, all pathways were ours.